D1527149

Tomorrow I Might Be Sausage

Tomorrow I Might Be Sausage: An Anthology in Four Seasons
First Edition

Casca Books
Copyright © 2024 by Michael Raysses
All rights reserved.

Some essays in the book were adapted from columns that appeared in *The Hammond Times*, *Vision* magazine and elsewhere, from 2002 to 2013.

For further information, please contact the author at michaelraysses@hotmail.com.

ISBN: 9798336892765

Artwork and photos courtesy of Michael Raysses
Cover design by Bruce Kluger/Midjourney

Tomorrow I Might Be Sausage
An Anthology in Four Seasons

Michael Raysses

CASCA BOOKS
CALIFORNIA

CONTENTS

For Beck

FOREWORD

August 11, 1989

Sitting at my kitchen table with a blank piece of paper and a Bic pen — whose greatest value until now has been to provide me with a cap to clean the inside of my ears with — I got this sneaking hunch that I'm the butt of some kind of practical joke. Unless you count a couple of bad checks, I'm not a writer. So being asked to come up with a foreword for a book that has yet to be written by a young man who tells me he's a writer seems a fool's errand. Am I putting imaginary carts in front of horses that aren't yet born? And what's a foreword, anyway?

   Truthfully, I got no idea what to write. When does someone you know who occasionally puts random sheets of paper into your hand and asks you to read them become a writer? Then again, now seems as good a time as any...

No matter. The aspiring author of the as—yet—unwritten book left me with this advice: write what I know. With that in mind, I'll say this: Still waters may run deep, but Michael's teaching me that swift waters can reach a surprising depth — they just do it in their own time.

Of one thing I am sure: his intention in writing whatever book he writes. It's something he would never have done if he thought reading it would be a waste of your time.

Anyway, I hope you enjoy it. I know I will, assuming I'm still alive when it's finally published. And if not, I'll ask for my money back.

—Tasso Bouboulakis

PREFACE

Dear Reader,

Just writing that greeting feels presumptuous to me—like, who am I to assume you'll actually show up, much less read this? This has long been an issue for me; thus, this preemptive explanation.

For me, writing requires an act of faith, a leap into a void of, arguably, my own creation. The way I figure it, if I can muster the courage to create an arbitrary empty space, I've got to believe I'm capable of filling that space with something worthwhile, something worthy of you, of your time and attention.

Something like this anthology.

And yet...

I wish I could tell you that I wrote this book for you. I also wish I could say that just writing that sentence made my hair grow in thicker while flattening my stomach. But that would instantly render me untrustworthy. That's because I wrote this book pretty much like I've written everything in my life: for me.

Since grade school, writing has been my way of making sense of the world by trying to prove an elusive truth: that I existed, that I was alive. Growing up, I wasn't entirely sure I belonged here, primarily because I was constitutionally incapable of seeing myself.

Consequently, when I began writing down my thoughts, it never occurred to me that what I'd written would be read by anyone else, except for maybe the occasional teacher. To be honest, that suited me just fine—because in addition to helping me make sense of the world, writing was how I kept myself company.

Over time, though, it also helped me to understand what I was feeling. Before then, some event would transpire and, despite being aware of it, I wouldn't know precisely how that moment landed in my head or in my heart. The ever-present option of a random pen and a stray piece of paper changed all that; and soon I was scribbling away, nurturing my budding sense of self-expression-as-self-exploration, a process I wasn't consciously aware of.

However, something I did become acutely mindful of at some point in my development was how a person or a thing could contain diametrically opposed forces within itself. That this phenomenon had an actual word that defined it—*duality*—elated me.

And duality never fit more snugly than when I first heard the timeless phrase "Greek to me" in Shakespeare's *Julius Caesar*, and eventually borrowed it for my writing. Being of Greek heritage, I was inspired by the fact that I'd found an expression that simultaneously represented the existence of something inscrutable—the "Greek"—but, as applied to me, something very familiar.

Thus, every essay in this book was written in the spirit of "Greek to Me," whether those words are spoken or not. With that sensibility firmly in hand, I concluded, I was free to explore duality's greatest expression: Life.

Because as we all know...

...life is a strange and wondrous thing.

Michael Raysses

August 24, 2024

Summer

Life, Art, and a Strategic Pause

Since the dawn of time, man has confronted Life's Big Questions (hereinafter referred to as LBQs). In prehistoric times, one of those LBQs was whether you were a fan of the saber-toothed tiger or the woolly mammoth. That query would eventually evolve into the modern-day cat-versus-dog issue. I was neither. Growing up, I was primarily preoccupied with one pressing LBQ: "What do I want to be when I grow up?"

The truth is, I wanted to be a Gas Station Man. Of course, this was back in the day when gas stations were only full-service, and you didn't have to consult your investment broker to fill your tank. But I eventually got bamboozled out of my pump-jockey longings by that cultural phenomenon that says if you manifest one dominant trait as a kid, then there's only one profession you're fit to do. And because I had the "gift of gab," I had to become a lawyer.

So I did. I practiced for a small private firm for whom I did one jury trial. I was reminded of it recently when I was cast as a lawyer in the TV show, *NYPD Blue*.

My firm represented a woman bitten by her land-lord's dog. A surefire loser, her case lingered like something stuck to our firm's shoe. Not surprisingly, being the youngest lawyer in the office, I inherited it. And because the judge was displeased at our inability to settle the matter, he unexpectedly moved the trial date up.

With little time to prepare, I frantically pored over the file, trying to cobble together something resembling a strategy. The most striking piece of evidence I found was a picture of the guilty canine, an aged Chihuahua named Waffles.

When I contacted our client, she barely remembered the case had even been filed. This was great, I reasoned; as a result of the bite in question, she was suffering short-term memory loss! But on speaking with her further, what became evident was that what she was really suffering from was terminal indifference.

The night before trial I memorized everything about the case. I anguished over the jurors I'd chosen; I wondered if I'd sounded stupid asking a group of adult men and women if they could return a verdict against someone named Waffles.

I arranged to meet my client outside the courtroom the next morning. As sweat rolled off my palms, I saw the opposing lawyer, and recognized him instantly: He looked as if he was holding a winning lottery ticket, and this case was his prize.

My client finally arrived. She was squat, as wide as she was tall, a human cube. She was also disheveled and ornery, a cranky demeanor that, for a brief moment, had me once again longing to be a Gas Station Man. But the gavel pounded, and the trial began.

In a series of surreal scenes that would've been more fitting in a John Waters movie than a courtroom, here's what I remember:

The landlord, an elderly gentleman, testified that Waffles was 22 years old at the time of the alleged bite, the canine equivalent of 140-plus years. In fact, Waffles was also blind, had cancer, and suffered from diseased gums. Mercifully, he had since died.

Thankfully, on cross-examination I got the landlord to admit that Waffles was technically ambulatory before he died. Even more important, he confessed that Waffles did indeed have at least one tooth, so that he was physically capable of inflicting the bite in question, canine gingivitis notwithstanding.

My optimism about our cause, however, skidded badly when it came time for my client to take the stand. While she was being sworn in, she raised her left hand instead of her right. The bailiff barely winced, coolly telling her to raise her "other right hand." The jury loved that.

Things quickly got worse. My client testified that the dog bite was actually a nick. No gaping wound, no lingering pain, no suffering. Just something akin to a paper cut, inflicted by a blind, near-toothless mutt named for his favorite breakfast treat.

But the highlight of the trial came during my closing argument. Newly invigorated by my prosecutorial prowess, intoxicated by the very sound of my oratory, I approached the jury box and made a dramatic, sweeping gesture with my hand, wholly unaware that as I did so, the inside of the cheap pen I was holding came out of its casing, then sailed across the courtroom, where it lodged in the paneling on the far wall. As it did so, I saw all twelve jurors carefully follow its arc, their heads swiveling in unison as if chained together. When it

3

landed, I could've sworn it actually made that *boing* sound you hear in cartoons.

The jurors all gazed back at me with a communal *Did you just see what we saw?* expression.

If I'm going to be honest, what I wanted to do at that moment was cackle at the absurdity of it all, pondering aloud at how we'd all found ourselves in this place, at this time, debating the merits (or lack thereof) of this ridiculous case.

But instead, I followed my instincts, and practiced what I can only call *the art of the strategic pause*. I leaned on the railing in front of the jury box, and with great gravity, I hung my head as if weighing the magnitude of some shimmering eternal truth that I was about to reveal. In all candor, what I was really doing was allowing the laughter within to roll over me. Then, as it passed, I looked straight into the eyes of each and every juror and asked them to find in favor of my client.

Two hours later, they returned a resounding "not guilty" for the defendant. I was despondent, of course. But amazingly, the judge congratulated me.

"Son, if I'd been the jury foreman, we'd have rendered a verdict for the defendant in three minutes," he said. "You got these people to deliberate for two hours. That's something."

Not surprisingly, I quit being an attorney shortly after that. Time was flying by, I reasoned, and I felt like I had nothing to show for its passage. Acting, I further surmised, might provide that elusive something I was longing for.

Looking back, I'm not sure it ever did. But I will tell you this: During that episode of *NYPD Blue*, when the actress playing the judge ruled in my character's favor, I felt a genuine rush—I just don't know if it came from that part of me that *was* a lawyer or that part of me that *is* an actor.

On my way home from the shoot I stopped at a restaurant that served breakfast, all day and night. When I asked the waitress whether the place had any specialties, she asked me if I liked waffles. As the image of an ancient Chihuahua came flooding in I started to answer her—then I strategically paused.

"It's complicated," I said.

All Golf and No Play

Work and play are such an innocuous pair of words; seemingly unrelated activities, each one offering a prism through which we view aspects of our lives. It's interesting how the relationship between the two words changes when you consider them conflicting forces, so that "work and play" ostensibly becomes "work *versus* play."

Growing up, that is exactly how I saw the two. For me, summer equaled vacation, and vacation equaled play. But my dad had this crazed notion that summer meant work. So, every year we revisited the classic confrontation of good versus evil under the guise of work versus play.

One summer, my dad went so far as to get me an interview with the caddy master at the local country club. In my head, I imagined him looking like Ricardo Montalbán. He'd offer me a grape Nehi, I decided, as we sat in the cool repose of his Corinthian leather-appointed office. He'd observe that I was preternaturally cultured beyond my years, and that my services would best be utilized in the position of poolside pizza taster.

But, alas, the caddy master looked nothing like Ricardo Montalbán. In fact, he was a grim young man with a pockmarked face and all the warmth of an ice pick in January. I nicknamed him Captain Happy.

After sailing through the interview (I could audibly speak) and passing the rigorous physical examination (I could walk upright), I got the job. I was a beginning caddy, the lowest of the low, earning $2.25 per round, while starting at the crack of dawn.

So the next morning I got up while it was still dark, and rode my trusty Schwinn five-speed with the ram-horn handlebars to the caddy shack. I even brought a pen and paper to compile the list of caddies for the morning. I put my name first on that list. Life was good. For an instant.

My very first official caddy assignment was for one of four businessmen. I'll never forget the look on my guy's face when I told him I was his caddy. He looked at me like I was his mail-order bride, but I didn't match my picture. When I saw his bag, I understood why—it was as big as I was. When I tried to sling it over my shoulder, the bottom dragged on the ground. But that was the least of my worries.

You see, I knew nothing about golf. If ignorance was bliss, I was in a state of nirvana.

Until the first hole.

I didn't know that I was supposed to follow the ball's trajectory once my guy hit his tee shot, so when he said, "Did you see that shot?" I thought he was brag-ging. When he repeated the question, I replied, "No—did you?" In that moment, let's just say that I redefined the phrase "teed off."

A few holes later, all four players were preparing to putt. While they clumped together for a morning beer, I walked up on the green, only to find four quarters strewn on the grass. Finders, keepers, I thought, as I methodically pocketed them, knowing exactly how many games of pinball they'd buy.

When the four returned, they couldn't find their "markers," a term I'd never heard before. They must've thought I was legally insane when I denied any knowledge of them—my hands thrust deep into my pockets, the defiant jingle of the tainted cargo giving proof to my lie.

But rock-bottom came on the ninth hole. I was "tending the pin"—you know, that long, thin metal thingy with the flag on top. I was standing next to it, holding it while my guy putted. In a perfect world, as my guy's ball glided toward the hole, I would lift the pin from the cup, allowing the ball to drop into it. But as his ball rolled toward the hole and I pulled, the pin wouldn't budge. I pulled harder, to no avail. I looked up—the ball was zipping straight to the cup. I gripped the pin with both hands and yanked so hard the entire cup apparatus came out of the ground. The ball hit its levitated base and bounced into a sand trap.

No one said a word, but if looks could kill, my guy would still be serving hard time.

I set a precedent that day: my party ditched me between the front and back nine. This didn't bother me a bit. They had all the joy of the Four Horsemen of the Apocalypse. In fact, I noticed that about all the golfers I saw there: they flailed, they cursed, and they took no pleasure in playing.

After that, Captain Happy relegated me to caddying exclusively for elderly women with hair the color of gunmetal. They'd start a round of golf on a Monday morning and finish sometime Tuesday afternoon.

I'd been demoted for sure, but what I instantly noticed about my new Golden Girl assignees was that they were the only ones who actually enjoyed themselves on the course. They chattered constantly; they laughed with abandon, ribbing each other good-naturedly for their errant shots. Maybe it wasn't a function of their age that made them take so long. Maybe they were just having too much fun to rush things. Inadvertently, I had found my people. They knew *summer was for play*.

Oddly enough, caddying also introduced me to the notion of pondering work and play and the idea that they could, indeed, intersect—that they didn't need to be opposing forces. That bud of a thought would eventually take full bloom years later, when I found myself impassioned by certain things of my own—like performing in front of people, or reading and writing, and wondering how I could get someone to pay me to do them.

Although my career as a caddy was short-lived, I did learn an invaluable lesson (beyond becoming a bad-ass mahjong player, that is): While the gap between what you can expect in life and what you actually get is often wide, reconciling that gap is something we must work hard at. For me, it is life's ultimate act of play.

When False Alarms Ring True

Ever since I was a kid, I've been obsessed with permission. No doubt this was because, back then, so much of what I was able to do was qualified by getting the parental go-ahead to do it. The phrase "May I have permission to…" was as rote as my use of "please" and "thank you," the staples of the day.

The funny thing is, I've never been able to acknowledge this fixation, even to myself, until recently. I've behaved like a man who is not dependent on anyone to grant me permission to do anything, when for most of my life just the opposite has been true. Permission was the key that unlocked the door to my freedom, and for far too many years, it was something I refused to carry.

Not surprisingly, my introduction to the idea that permission lived outside of me and was granted by people of power came from my parents, the initial purveyors of authority. And as I grew older, they extended that status to other adults, regardless of their qualifications. In my parents' minds, I was still just a kid and thus had to constantly defer to other adults. Why? Because, quite simply, they were adults and assumably they knew better.

This was a system I accepted for a few years, though at some point it ceased to fit me. I could feel it as

10

oppressively as a garment I'd outgrown, leaving me tugging and pulling at myself to break loose. My efforts were rewarded one night in the most unsuspecting way.

Growing up, my family spent a lot of time at church. We weren't particularly pious; for us, church was a major socio-cultural hub. My parents sang in the choir, and my sisters and I went to Sunday school, more regularly than religiously. All of this in addition to the numerous dinners and dances held there.

I was at one of those dances sometime during my tenth year. At that age, those dances overwhelmed me. Live music, Greek dancing, and people eating and drinking with an abandon that was so palpable it had its own scent. All of this churned into a smoke-tinged kaleidoscope that drove me wild with possibilities I couldn't yet fully grasp.

On this specific night I'd grown bored of dodging between flying feet and the clutched hands of the dancers that crowded the floor, so I retreated to a corner where I could just watch. As I scanned the room, everyone was waist-deep in celebration. Everyone, that is, except the church sexton, Mr. Kouras. A cold slab of marble, Mr. Kouras was the prototypical adult-to-be-respected I'd been weaned on. Even back then, I was sure he was born looking older than he was; and because the nature of his job was to fix things, he was always looking for something that was broken.

Well, at this particular gathering the building's boiler malfunctioned, and the smell of smoke began wafting into the hall. Mr. Kouras sniffed the air suspiciously, and then, with all the gravity of a Secret Service agent looking for a stray bullet to take, he strode to the fire alarm in the back of the hall, close to where I was positioned.

It was one of those old-fashioned fire alarms, the kind that was embedded into the wall, behind a locked pane of glass. On the wall, next to the glass, was a small mallet on a chain. In case of a fire, you were supposed to take the mallet off its hook, smash the glass, and sound the alarm. But the chain on this particular mallet had broken, and someone had placed it inside the glass compartment next to the alarm itself.

Mr. Kouras quickly reached the alarm, and in an indescribable fit of lunatic panache, he opened the pane that shielded the alarm. He then took the mallet out, firmly closed the glass gate, smashed it with the mallet, reached in and rang the alarm, calmly placing the mallet back inside the gate, next to the pulsating alarm.

In that moment, it was as if I'd witnessed a law of nature being broken—like I'd seen something falling up when it should've fallen down. I looked around to see if anyone else had witnessed what I'd just seen—*an adult had done something wantonly stupid!*

With that event, in that very instant, the universe was basically reordered. I no longer struggled for permission to subvert my parents' approach to authority. From that moment forward, respect was going to have to be earned for it to be exhibited. Nothing felt more liberating than that. Growing up in the sixties, questioning authority became *de rigueur.* This event put a face on that fact.

It wasn't long after that I was at my cousin's house when my aunt made us lunch. As we sat down to eat, I stared at the cup of canned vegetable soup she always served—soggy shadows of what were once vegetables slowly drowning in a pasty pool of leaden broth. Before, whenever I protested her offering, my aunt prevailed by dint of her authority as someone "who knew what was good for me." But the vision of Mr. Kouras and his little mallet eroded her clout in a flash. When my aunt forced her hand, I stiffened, and countered with a pair of folded arms and a knowing smirk. No canned vegetable soup ever passed my lips again.

A couple of years later when I became an altar boy, I'd see Mr. Kouras with great frequency. I never told him that I saw what he'd done that day, and how it gave me permission to think for myself. And I'm glad I didn't because today I know that he didn't give me that permission. I did. And it's something I have to remind myself of every day.

Which is alarmingly Greek to me.

Innocence Misplaced

"Zorba the Greek wasn't."
—*My Uncle Tasso, noting that the most famous Greek character of my lifetime was portrayed on screen by Anthony Quinn, a man of Mexican descent.*

In the timeless battle of East versus West, the place where those two polar opposites often meet most directly is arguably Greece. There, the mysticism of the East runs head-on into the modernity of the West.

Growing up Greek-American, my role model for all things Greek was the protagonist in Nikos Kazantzakis' novel, *The Life and Times of Alexis Zorba* (and the 1964 film adaptation, *Zorba the Greek*). Since Zorba was somewhat of a Lothario, he naturally also became my role model for interacting with women. (Historically speaking, Zorba was the best I could come up with. Although I admired the philosopher Plato as a very bright guy, all of his relationships were, well, platonic.) But choosing Zorba's example imposed an unwitting burden—he knew so much, and I knew so very little.

"God has a very big heart," Zorba observes in the movie, "but there is one sin He will not forgive: if a woman calls a man to her bed and he will not go! I know because a very wise old Turk told me."

14

The year was 1974. The sexual revolution was raging across the country. I was a freshman in college and a not-so-conscientious objector in the upheaval that had engulfed campuses nationwide. I very intentionally had taken up residence in a dormitory that, the year prior to my freshman year, *Playboy* magazine had rated the third best party dorm in the country. I was there to contribute whatever I could to get us to number one.

It was a typical Saturday night. I was lying on my bunk bed, recovering from a night out in which I'd drunk too much beer in too little time, when a girl walked by my open door looking for someone who lived on my floor. I told her that he was gone for the weekend, then asked her why she was looking for him. It turned out that she needed a place to sleep for the night. Coincidentally, my roommate was gone for the evening, too. Innocently, I offered her his bed. Naturally, she declined. But she came in anyway, and after a spirited three-hour conversation, she asked if my original offer was still open.

It was.

Her name was Marianne. I got her a tee-shirt to sleep in and left the room so she could change. When I came back in it was time for bed. I had this urge to kiss her, which I did very chastely—on the cheek. I turned out the light and climbed up onto the top of the bunk bed, which ran perpendicular to the lower bed she was sleeping on. As I settled in, I looked down at her and thought, *Wow—there's a girl in my room!*

Content with that realization, I put my hands behind my head, ready to sleep. Just as I was about to nod off, Marianne's voice came wafting up from below.

"Michael, I'm *really* hot!"

So I did what I thought any red-blooded man would do: I slid off my bed onto hers, skipping like a stone, my momentum carrying me over to the far wall, where I opened a window, scampered back up into my bed, and promptly fell asleep.

The next morning we awoke and went our separate ways without incident. Minutes later, I was eating breakfast with friends in the dormitory cafeteria as I recounted the prior night's events, in no specific order, and just as I got to the part where Marianne said, "Michael, I am really hot," the air suddenly grew thick and sticky. I heard those words anew, but in slow-motion, reverberating with newfound meaning.

I'd committed Zorba's unforgivable sin—a woman had called me to her bed and I didn't go! I dropped my fork mid-bite with a clang and raced to her room.

When I got there, she invited me in, and soon we were intensely making out. Just as I started thinking about birth control, I was visited by Zorba's ghost, making me feel the need to say something manly and experienced (which is to say, things I had no relationship with whatsoever). So as casually as I could muster, I offered the following:

"You know, I don't have any raincoats…" Her look to me said, "We're in the middle of foreplay and you're worried about precipitation?!"

At that point, Marianne literally took matters into her own hands and removed my glasses, rendering me legally blind. Having miraculously decoded my reference to raincoats as a concern about birth control, she reached into her closet and pulled out what looked like a small orange Frisbee. "Don't worry," she said casually, "I've got this."

Not wanting to appear ignorant, I assumed the Frisbee was a diaphragm. When I asked her if she used it, she replied, "Yes, every day." At that bit of news, my eyes got bigger than the Frisbee itself, as I asked her to show me how she used it. She held it up to my face, where I saw something I didn't expect: the days of the week in small print. It was a birth control pill dispenser.

She was on the pill! I was in heaven! Damn the torpedoes, full speed ahead!

Coincidentally, at that point, "speed" became the operative word...

If my life were an impressionistic film, we would have cut to a shot of an unmanned fire hose, only smaller, as it flailed madly about. Then, even the modern-day miracle of time-lapse photography couldn't have captured the love act that day, it flashed by so quickly. We finished, and in my most Zorba-like tone, I asked her if she would like to do it again. She looked at me as if to say, "*Again* implies that we've done it once— and if so, I wasn't here for that."

By my body's warp-speed count, we did it two more times in less time than it takes a world-class sprinter to run one hundred meters. By the time we were done, I was channeling Zorba, full-on. But when I suggested that we get together again, I was met by a stillborn silence. Without a word, Marianne informed me in no uncertain terms that there would be no sequel to the debacle that had just transpired.

As I slunk back to my room, I realized that I didn't so much lose my virginity that day, I'd *misplaced* it, largely by not living up to Zorba's example. Thankfully, though, he left me with a quote that allowed me to go forward, into the world of women and love:

"*And as for women, you make fun of me that I love them. How can I not love them? They're such poor, weak creatures. And they give you all they've got.*"

For me, it doesn't get any more Greek than that.

Terra Cognita: Landscape of an Avoidance Behaviorist

It is an amazing stroke of good fortune that I was born into a Greek-American family. Beyond enabling me to sit through countless viewings of the movie *My Big Fat Greek Wedding*, my lineage lent me an affinity for the ancient Greeks and their timeless aphorisms. "Know Thyself" is one such adage, just beating out my second favorite ancient Greek saying, "Just Know Thyself." This was actually my favorite until research revealed that it was nothing more than the first slogan for what was an ancient Greek marketing campaign for Nike's emerging line of knee-high sandals.

But I digress...

Beyond its applicability as a marketing device, the saying's significance is of infinite value because it speaks to the acquisition of self-knowledge. But the phrase begs much deeper analysis: what exactly constitutes self-knowledge? Is it the golden ideal of understanding human thought, behavior, and the morals that shape those things? Or does self-knowledge refer to a less lofty perch, perhaps a baseline awareness of one's innate inability to wear stripes without appearing to be a few pounds overweight?

For me, though, a timeless warrior in a battle that has no end, I interpret it to mean that my responsibility is to know who I am on a day-to-day basis; how I am going to react in most any given situation; and not only how I have done so in the past, but how I am likely to do so in the future, given who it is I have become up until that moment. This is what I have come up with:

Charitably speaking, I am what I call an Avoidance Behaviorist. But before you pelt me with knee-jerk judgments about my status as such, allow me a little backstory, if you will.

I've been writing this essay for the past two weeks now. I've hunkered down, fully prepared to confront the enemy blank page. No sooner did I set pen to paper, though, than I noticed the floor around my desk was really messy. Being an absolute stickler for a pristine work environment, I laid down my arms and called a truce while I corralled the dust bunnies that had mutated into what looked more like dust buffaloes. When cleanliness was restored, I returned to the task, only to realize it was time to go to work. Oh, the humanity…

I awakened the next day, fully intending to resume work on this piece. But then it hit me—I don't write particularly well on even-numbered days ending in the letter "y." In a fit of lunatic inspiration, I went to the Museum of Dental Hygiene for a little stimulation; and though I didn't get what I bargained for, I left the building feeling more minty fresh than a man has the right to feel.

The next morning I confronted the Great White Void yet again. This time, though, I set aside extra time, just in case a rogue band of feral dust buffaloes should invade my office. (No such luck.) As I fingered my lucky dental floss (a memento from my trip to the museum), I set my steely gaze on the horizon of the page and embarked on the opening sentence. That is, until I noticed the date—July 12th—the birthday of Curly Joe DeRita, the American actor/comedian who played the final Curly in The Three Stooges. Not having seen a Three Stooges film in years, I felt the need to pay homage to the bonds that time and space had strained. So I did the noble and just thing—I watched a chronological marathon of the Stooges' shorts.

Unfortunately, though, it was hours before DeRita appeared on screen, and by the time he had, I was too exhausted to write. Besides, now it was time to go to work again—curse my need for food and rent!

For you hawk-eyed readers noticing a pattern while feeling a creeping sense of sanctimony lap at your feet, I know you're thinking that I am some rank procrastinator, a laggard of the lowest order. No, I am chronicling inchoate genius for you, right before your very eyes. Because all great art—no, all of humankind—is dependent on the stalwart efforts of an elite class heretofore unacknowledged by the general population. We are not dawdlers and stragglers—we are Avoidance Behaviorists. History bears our inimitable imprint!

Michelangelo, famed fifteenth-century artist/notary public who painted the Sistine Chapel, only did so to avoid installing shelves in his wife's closet. Christopher Columbus was supposed to give sailing lessons to a bratty Spanish prince when he opted to find the New World instead. Mother Teresa? An inveterate Avoidance

Behaviorist, she was en route to getting her MBA when she decided that dedicating her life to administering to the poor and sick was more appealing than completing her master's thesis.

A world without avoidance behavior is incomprehensible to me. Without it, humanity has no future. Here is why: Having children is quite possibly the apotheosis of avoidance behavior, and thank God for that fact. To change this system now would undermine the evolutionary imperative of propagating the species. What better, more ironic way is there to avoid confronting one's own life than by creating the ultimate distraction—a miniature version of yourself?

I rest my case.

As a demigod in the ageless pantheon of Avoidance Behavior, I don't ask for much by way of obeisance. Rather, as you venture out into the world, use the flinty dedication of responsibility-challenged deities like myself as a template.

And to those who think me a sham just because I actually completed this column, you should know I have an impending deadline on an unfinished book proposal that made all this possible. And if that's Greek to you, just ask yourself this—isn't there something else you should be doing right about now?

In Praise of Shit

"I've yet to see a fertilizer salesman go belly up."
—*My Uncle Tasso on the topic of shit.*

These are tough times. I don't care where you sit on the sociopolitical spectrum; it doesn't matter what your economic station in life is—this is a rough-and-tumble era.

If you're a Tea-Bagger (sorry, if the epithet fits, wear it), there are simply way too many crazies out there who care about hare-brained notions like the environment and the sanctity of the individual in the face of an ever-burgeoning corporate kleptocracy to go around. If you're a member of that slightly less crazed bunch that I refer to as the Radical UnLeft (there is nothing "right" about them), the same broad criticisms will no doubt apply. And if by some long shot you're a member of that class of people who are rapidly qualifying for inclusion on the endangered species list known as liberals, lefties, commies, etc., you will arguably agree that things have devolved to such a place that the phrase "It's all gone to shit" has taken hold with hermetic strength. And stench.

All of which I'd find alarming if it weren't for one simple fact:

I love shit.

You know, crap, cow pies, road apples, poop, stool, doody, that shit. I know what you're thinking—this man has gone batshit, which, given the point I'm making here, strikes me as perversely congruent. But in a time and place in which nothing and no one seems to be what they represent themselves to be, I find, um, relief, in dung's unalloyed nature. More than anything I know of, it is exactly what it seems to be. And if you're not moved by its physical traits, just take a deep breath—if that doesn't bring a tear to your eye, step on it and go for a walk. The court of public opinion will let you in on the obvious.

If pressed, though, I suppose I don't actually love shit. I love *the idea* of it: that there is something in this world that is so purely what it is as to banish all discourse of what it might otherwise arguably be.

Which, to me, is the shit.

Linguistically speaking, though, shit is a word of a thousand feces. What other item can be taken or given with such relative ease, without ever literally moving? It can be little, deep, or tough. You can get it together, lose it, shoot it, or have it for brains. It can fly, sometimes hitting the proverbial fan. It can put a pig into a state of delirium, though you wouldn't want to be upstream on any creek that shares its name without a paddle. And woe to the person who can't distinguish it from Shinola, a brand of shoe polish that was popular in the mid-twentieth century.

This is actually where, for me, shit loses its charm and takes on its most feculent state. For all of its conceptual malleability, its greatest misuse has been as a tool for agents of what I like to call the Anti-Shit-for-

Shinola conspiracy. This group seeks to deceive people by overexposing them to metaphorical shit, causing them to suffer what I call "fecal fatigue," losing the ability to tell the difference between shit and its opposite.

As dated a reference as it must seem in this age of the ephemeral, I think the years 2000 to 2008 are key. For my money, that was an eight-year blizzard of dung bunnies, started by an act of unprecedented political thievery, from which only more dung flowed. Governmental programs whose titles were abject lies (think "No Child Left Behind") gave way to military strategies aimed at inappropriate targets cloaked in names that aspired to Shock and Awe, but only gave way to Shame and Disgust.

But even in the wake of the political cow pie that was the George W. Bush administration, one could arguably point to shit's ability to fertilize the ground it fell on. For the first time in history, the party that rose to oppose those who had been in power offered up not only a woman but also a man of color as its primary candidates. Wasn't that progress?

As it turns out, shit no. The President seemingly took office on a mandate of desired change from a status quo that was poop personified. But he proved all too willing to take the crap his ideological opponents proffered, all of which resulted in the governmental dump embodied by the subsequent issue of the debt ceiling and its theoretical resolution.

For the first time, our government was reduced to using a tactic I used as a desperate teenager—the use of the word "super" to mask efforts that were anything but. When I was guilty of some misdeed, I would be super-contrite, pledging super-attention to not repeat my infraction, all offered with super-sincerity. Seeing the powers that be offer up a super-Congress to address an issue as pressing as the debt ceiling, knowing it was there all along, was nothing short of super-shitty.

A steady diet of figurative excrement can't help but inflict long-term damage. George W. Bush begat Sarah Palin, who begat Rick Perry and Michelle Bachmann. For me, this wasn't about liberal or conservative, or left versus right. It was about shit from Shinola. It was about being deluged with crap to such an extent that we lost the ability to tell the difference anymore, so that when someone places a steaming bowl of something in front of us and invites us to eat it, we do because we don't know any better. Or because we no longer think we have any choice in the matter.

But we do. I, for one, am sick of this crap—*I know shit from Shinola, and you do, too!*

So next time someone or some entity tries to pawn off some symbolic Shinola on you, push back and tell them you know shit.

It's your doody.

Paddling to Sanity

"So is Hell."
—*My Uncle Tasso's response to hearing me extol
Los Angeles for always being hot.*

I'm probably the last guy in the world to credibly comment about the world's hot spots. Beyond the fact that I'm not well-traveled, I have an innate disdain for the concept of "hot"—that which is socially aspired to, culturally endorsed, or sexually alluring. My natural antipathy for all things thermodynamic is further buttressed by the awareness that even if something achieves "hotness," it will inevitably at some point lose its heat and ultimately become cold. As in devoid of life. As in dead. Call me old school but I still cling to this raft we call life with considerable enthusiasm.

Thus, I'm a devotee of cool; it's timeless and without the pedestrian considerations that inform hot's equation. And though there's a collective aspect to what constitutes "cool," the older I get the more I recognize that cool is essentially something very personal: it is what you deem it to be, separate and apart from any communal ideas surrounding it. It is something both to aspire to and to embody; it is protean and fluid. And it expresses itself in some very strange and unexpected ways.

To wit:

Ping-pong.

(Full disclosure: I didn't see one second of the recent Olympics, and though I'm told that ping-pong was prominently displayed and a wonder to behold, its appearance within this column is sheer coincidence.)

(Fuller disclosure: I don't want to be suspect for jumping on any bandwagon or topic that approaches "hot." That would definitely *not* be cool.)

(Fullest disclosure: I fucking love ping-pong.)

Recently, I was mired in what I will charitably refer to as "my morning routine," a seemingly benign behavioral trope of physical exercise, coffee, a *New Yorker* magazine, and sitting in front of my local Starbucks, watching the river of humanity flow by, while trolling for meaningful human connection. But since I'm the man who put the "rut" in "routine," at some point my regimen became toxic, forcing me to strike out in search of a new adventure to break its stranglehold.

So, one morning, after some exercise, I took my coffee and my *New Yorker* and found a new vantage point from which to watch said river of humanity flow by (hey, change comes in increments!): a small outdoor mall here in Malibu. There I found an interesting configuration—some comfy outdoor furniture had been loosely arrayed in close proximity to, of all things, a ping-pong table.

It looked at once out of place yet somehow totally at one with its setting. I was drawn to it like a moth to a flame. That is, assuming that moth had played the game as a kid and in college, enthralled by its sublime mixture of the physical, mental, and social.

From that perch, over the last month, this is what I've learned, in no particular order: Asking a total stranger to play ping-pong is a lot like asking them if they'd like to unexpectedly visit some deep, dark part of their past. Instantly. With someone they've never seen before. Which is not necessarily to say that they thought playing would be a bad thing or that they declined without reason. As the offerer, I learned to be ready for all manner of response, the most frequent being a variation of the shaky but qualified, "Okay, but I really suck."

Secondly, kids like to be taught—you just have to be willing to be patient and supportive. Every morning, a group of children of varying ages would spill onto the couch and chairs, fresh from the ocean where they were learning to surf. Desperate for someone to play with, I offered up a game to any takers. Although most were new to the sport, they were eager to learn. And over the course of the last month, a couple of them remarkably improved their game.

Thirdly, advancing age is a great deceiver to the casual observer. I wish I had a dollar for every young man or boy who somewhat smugly accepted my offer to play, only to lose to a middle-aged bald guy whom they didn't see as posing any kind of challenge. Without hubris, it was fascinating to watch these buckets full of bravado slowly drain, point by point, until they were empty, their paddles surrendered in silent retreat, with barely a muted "thanks."

Although I reaffirmed some forgotten lessons as the result of this last go-around with the game—e.g., that I love competition within a structured format, and that people are rarely what they seem—while also learning something new (never, ever play in sandals), I gleaned the most from just watching and listening.

I could tell whether a person was going to play just by the way they addressed the table. Some would glance at it, then quickly look away for fear of being seen, only to have their eyes return to gaze more fixedly, even if just for an instant. It conveyed a dynamic reminiscent of a lover reconsidering what was, while dealing with the implicit what might be should they stop and swing a paddle.

Some walked by with nary a look, though their fingers grazed the table's top to the very end, letting go only when they had to, betraying some deep subterranean desire. They'd return on their way out, their fingers still outstretched in desperation, as they glanced around nervously. And even those who refused to look its way or touch it communicated no less effectively—whatever was, assuming there was something at all, was now over.

I knew my relationship with that table had turned a corner when someone saw me in the local drugstore, pointed at me, and said, "You're the ping-pong guy!"

The summer is soon over, and with it my tenure as "the ping-pong guy." I'll still play from time to time, but the mornings of coffee and a *New Yorker*—all consumed with one eye on any stranger walking by a table as their fingers dance atop its smooth surface, tapping out a Morse code of "Wanna play?"—are numbered.

It's time for some new routines and to take the lessons of the table out into the world beyond. Now that will definitely be *cool*.

Fair Enough

When I was a kid, the circus came to an adjoining town. It set up camp at the Hammond Civic Center, a cavernous monolith that housed all manner of events designed to snag a young boy's fancy: rock concerts with stacks of Marshall amplifiers, and the Valhalla of public attractions, professional wrestling.

Unfortunately, those events weren't free, and the little discretionary income we had was earmarked for our annual vacation to what was known as the Greek Riviera. Unlike its French counterpart, our holiday retreat was nothing more than a cluster of ramshackle cottages so dilapidated that even mosquitoes stayed out for fear of their imminent collapse.

Its saving grace was that it was just a scenic stroll through the woods from the life-affirming shore of Lake Michigan; there, the visual clang of water so blue pounding against sand so white was mediated by the sonic swirl of the tall grass that sang as it swayed in the wind that whipped off the water.

With money being tight, we were relegated to events that were primarily "cost-effective" (read: free). This meant attending a stream of concerts by singers and musicians whose own families had long since forgotten that they'd ever played or sang. It also meant going to lectures given by people who'd traveled somewhere and documented every aspect of the trip by raising a cheap camera with a shaky hand, only to return home where they could give a free chat at the local library or church hall. Inevitably, these people shared one fatal trait: they stuttered. Which, in a way, was eerily consistent with the zeitgeist: out-of-focus pictures taken by a tremulous hand *should* have a stammering narrator, if only to illuminate comedy's darker corners.

And when we'd exhausted live entertainment as a source of constructive distraction, we went high-tech. "High-tech," circa the mid-sixties, meant a reel-to-reel movie projector, a bed sheet strung across a bare dining room wall, and whatever film the local library had available. (To this day I can't hear the word "nocturnal" without reflexively mouthing the words "Night Birds of the Serengeti," the title of the film that bluntly cured us from watching movies at home as a panacea for our boredom.)

From my perspective, though, the best remedy for our ennui was the county fair. It was circus-lite. And though it didn't have the exotic heft that the Big Top wielded, did I mention it was free?

One year, I went multiple times. I hitched rides with various friends' families after negotiating consecutive advances on my allowance, transactions that were harder to complete than qualifying for a loan from the World Bank, or so it felt.

The great thing about going to the county fair multiple times within a week was that I got to establish a deep, meaningful rapport with all the booth-keepers and operators, some of whom even had teeth. The guys that ran the Ring Toss? They recognized me by my face—oh, and by how close I had come to snagging the post that had a cigarette lighter, a gold watch, and a $10 bill, all as one prize. They were just waiting for my Hail Mary ring to lasso its lucre. Amazingly, that didn't happen.

There was an odd-looking couple that managed the milk bottle target range; coincidentally, they themselves were bottle-shaped, with pallid skin the color of sour milk. We became so close that they even counseled me on which cluster of bottles to aim for, a courtesy I didn't see them extend to anyone else.

But the ultimate perk of regular attendance was meeting the shepherd of the Shetland ponies. Clearly, he had an eye for talent. In me he saw unlimited potential. In me he saw someone who was kind, gentle, and entrepreneurial. In me he saw a leader—of Shetland ponies. So he offered me a job, touring with the fair.

I reasoned that I'd clear it with my parents by framing it as the ultimate example of work-study. I'd work while studying the various cuisines the fair offered—say, contrasting and comparing the crunchy delight of glazed popcorn balls with the deep-fried decadence of a corn dog drowning in mustard so luminous it looked like liquid sunlight.

And the best part of it was that it wouldn't interfere with my other, less significant life. You know, the one where I slept in my bed, woke up, ate breakfast, went to school, came home, did my chores, ate dinner, washed the dishes, did my homework, watched TV, and then went to bed. *That* life.

No, this experience would take the straw of my life

and spin it into gold for my budding career as a Miniature-Equine Field Associate. Once I'd convinced my dad that one supported the other, I'd be off and running. And as soon as school would let out for the summer, I'd join the fair full-time. I'd be smart as a whip, and willing as the wind to go wherever the ponies went, doing what had to be done.

There'd be no pile of dung too pungent for my shovel, no aged bale of hay too loose for me to gather. And for all my efforts, I'd get to tour the great state of Indiana, seeing its crowned heads firsthand. Towns with sensuous tags like French Lick. Or bergs with burly names like Gnaw Bone.

And whilst touring those places I'd interact with a rogues' gallery of characters, the most compelling of whom was the bearded lady who went by the name of Stan when he/she wasn't ensconced in his/her patch-work tent, on display for all to marvel at.

Alas, none of that happened. Although the offer was indeed made by the proprietor of the enchanted quadrupeds, no agreement, no magic, no incantation was going to result in my father allowing me to join the caravan for the summer.

But that's beside the point. Sitting here, writing, spinning fictive yarn with random threads of fact has been a journey unto itself, one I wish I'd been able to make as a kid. Although my tilt-a-whirl dreams never left home, what matters is that I can journey now whenever I want to. And that hopefully my trek can inspire yours.

That strikes me as fair enough.

Fall

Waiting for Tasso

Recently, while in the midst of penning this column, I became overwhelmed with an urge to speak with my Uncle Tasso. This was a watershed moment. Having exhausted all of my normal avoidance-behavior mechanisms, I was about to cross a line that could not be ignored: my dysfunction was no longer the expression of a lone wolf. I now had a prospective ally, one I hadn't spoken to in quite a while, a man who prefers to reach out in his own time and manner.

But in my feverish state, my impending deadline trumped decorum. As I punched his number into the receiver, I remembered that getting my Uncle on the phone is a lot like trying to raise someone who's in the witness protection program—it's a long shot at best. For one, he keeps an irregular schedule. Secondly, he loathes talking on the phone unless it's a measure of last resort. And as the phone continued ringing, I recalled that there was one more very practical obstacle to connecting with him this way: he doesn't have an answering machine, so in the event he wasn't home, I wouldn't even be able to tell him to return my call.

As the phone continued to ring, my thoughts drained into an unexpected pool of nostalgia; I couldn't remember the last time I'd made a phone call that wasn't routed to voicemail or an answering service. Not getting an answer at all was even rarer than the nearly extinct busy signal. And just as I was about to hang up, the rhythm of the phone ringing on the other end hypnotized me into staying on the line. Thusly lulled, I turned on the speaker phone and settled in.

As I sat there, I imagined the conversation we would have. For the uninitiated, my Uncle Tasso is not a blood relation. He is what's known as a "Greek uncle," which is to say his relationship to me is so close as to be that of blood without any of the lineal baggage. That Tasso just happens to be Greek only strengthens the seemingly blurry lines that connect us.

He is a philosopher: a combination of Yogi Berra and Socrates. He has the heart of a lion, the balls of a second-story man, and a mordant sense of humor that betrays a generosity that he goes to great lengths to conceal from the world at large. I have occasionally quoted him in my columns.

Whenever I get him on the phone, I'm always aware that he's smoking, which is funny because I've never seen him smoke in person. I can tell he's smoking, though, because of the rhythm of his breath, the express intake of air and the resultant exhale that is so pronounced that I can almost see the smoke rings floating above the kitchen table where he sits. And he must smoke non-filtered cigarettes because of the tell-tale spitting sound he occasionally makes into the receiver to expel a bit of wayward tobacco from his lips.

I would greet him and he would respond as he always does, by calling me "kid." In this instance, "Kid" becomes a proper name, one with a history that allows for many shades, both dark and light. Uncle Tasso would ask, "How's tricks?" I would respond, "Tricks are for kids," and we would be off and running.

Conversations with my Uncle are a living testament to the inexplicable value of those things that derive their worth simply by being there, by existing, without actually ever being used much.

Although the life of a retired, elderly working-class man can oftentimes be a blank canvas in search of form and color, Tasso betrays none of that amorphousness. In fact, I think one of his best tactics for remaining vital is something I learned as an actor: that he who lives best is one whose focus is outer-driven, with secondary awareness of self only in support of that notion.

Our imagined conversation continued. Inevitably, we would get around to my writing, and Tasso would ask about my latest effort. Not wanting him to feel any pressure around the fact that I'm using him as a catalyst—a muse, even—I blithely mention this column's theme: sowing seeds. As I do I can hear him turning it over in his mind the same way he tastes food when he is unsure of who cooked it. He takes another drag from his cigarette and blows out a thought.

"It invites a clichéd response." When I comment that every theme begs for a trite reply, he says, "Touché," and retreats deeper into thought. Then, finally, he counters, "Well, Kid, whatever you do, avoid agrarian references except for this one simple question: Are you the farmer or are you the field?"

This is classic Tasso. I don't know if his question is rhetorical or not, making me feel like I've been snared in a trap that upends me and leaves me dangling until I figure out whether or not to respond—and if I do, if I should try to conjure an answer worthy of the question. Finally, more out of desperation than cognition, I say, "Well, ideally, I'm both."

"Nice catch, Kid."

I hear him take a last pull from his butt, signaling the end of our talk. I think to ask him the source of his latest pearl of wisdom, but with Tasso it doesn't matter. The same man who likes to quote Plato is just as apt to cite the seventies TV show *Kung Fu* as a source of inspiration.

As always, he leaves me with the words "Don't be a stranger," which is his way of saying, "Stay in touch." I don't think I've ever told him, though, that I always hear it as a caution against becoming weirdly idiosyncratic.

But it doesn't matter because he never answered the phone. This conversation never took place. And still, somehow, I'm a better man for having been here.

Goodnight, Uncle Tasso. Thanks again—for nothing, for everything.

The Tale of a Tail and a Dog Named Dog

Not too long ago and not very far away lived a dog. The dog wasn't pedigreed and there was nothing remarkable about him beyond his status as the absolute embodiment of caninity—to wit: that thing which makes a dog a dog and not a table, though, technically speaking, they both have four legs. (If you keep in mind that this is a fable, these things will be much easier to accept.)

Our dog was such a dog that when it came time for his master to name him, only one name fit—Dog. And though it may have seemed to lack originality, it suited him more snugly than the fur he was coated in.

Despite all of life's inconsistencies and contradictions, Dog lived a very dog-like existence. He fetched more than his share of balls. He respectfully sniffed more than a few bitches. And he still didn't like it when his master watched him as he hunched and strained while doing his business, despite his beseeching looks for a little privacy.

Dog loved his body. He marveled at the way it looked when he saw his reflection in a puddle of rain after a thunderstorm. Most of all, he loved his tail. He remembered the day he discovered it. He'd been cleaning himself (why?—because he could, thank you very much) when he noticed it wagging seductively between his legs. With no thought whatsoever, he did what he felt irresistibly impelled to do—which is to say, he bit it. He then felt a searing bolt shoot up his spine. The pain rocked his head back and reminded him of a carnival sideshow attraction where his master had paid for the privilege of using a large mallet to send a metal object zooming up a steel rail where it struck a bell. *And people think dogs are weird*, Dog thought.

After becoming aware of his tail, Dog could think of nothing else. He was constantly sensing its presence in his life. When it swished flies away; when it flattened out as he chased a bird in the park; even when he was doing nothing more than lying on the floor, his legs splayed beneath him, his tail wagging to a rhythm that he didn't even hear, he was keenly conscious of it.

And then one day it happened.

He was really bored, and just to shake things up a bit, out of nowhere, he made one of those "woof" sounds. He knew it would drive his master to distraction, which it did, and if nothing else, it would get him to think about something other than his tail. But no sooner had his master finally asked his final "Who's a goo' boy?"—in a voice he typically used with babies and people of diminished capacity—than Dog's eyes irretrievably fell on his tail once again.

As much as he loved his tail, however, he began to be aware of the complexity of his connection to it. And that realization wasn't all good. Lately, for instance, he realized that sometimes the tail was wagging even if he didn't tell it to. Weren't he and the tail one? And, if not, where did he end and the tail begin? Dog began staring at it with a newfound intensity. For the first time ever, he decided that he was going to consciously exert dominion over the tail.

That's when Dog experienced the unimaginable.

As he looked at the tail it remained still, but inexplicably *he* moved. He felt as if he was going to faint, or at least sneeze, so great was his shock. And just when he remembered that there was a new family of squirrels living in his favorite tree out back, it happened again— *the tail wagged him.* And for everything Dog didn't know—e.g., what in God's name his master meant when he said "speak"—he knew that the tail should never wag the dog.

I can relate to Dog. These days, I walk around shaking my head with amazement—I feel as if we are all living in a world where the tail is wagging the dog. We are the dog; technology is the tail. We've lost sight of the fact that the tail is just an evolutionary creation there to complement the life of the being to which it is attached.

And the day we lose that perspective is a day to mourn the loss of our reason, because once that happens, any number of insane and inane conclusions are possible. We can strike terror in the hearts of others as a means of allaying our own sense of fear. We can desecrate the environment at will and fool ourselves into thinking it is necessary in the name of economic prosperity. And, on the most personal level, we can enslave ourselves to gadgets designed to facilitate communication and deceive ourselves into believing that we are more connected and more in touch than ever before.

If there was a postscript to the above fable, I am certain that in it Dog would release his consternation over his experience with the tyrannical tail, confident in the knowledge that all he had to do to reassert order was to relax into himself and his caninity.

Why?

Because he can.

The End of the Line

It's been said that youth is wasted on the young. I've always felt that one of youth's benefits has been consistently overlooked—that you're basically an empty vessel. Thus, everything you encounter, everything you experience, fills you up.

When I was a kid I was a head-to-toe tabula rasa, drawn to activities that I knew nothing about. For instance, one day I decided to become a pole vaulter, which, if not admirable, at least cleared the bar of my ignorance standard with flying colors (pun intended). I wasn't strong enough or fast enough, and the best trait in support of my effort was that I barely weighed one-hundred pounds—how hard could it be to get me airborne?

As it turned out, damn near impossible. Beyond not being able to muster the requisite speed or having the necessary upper-body strength, I also lacked the most important attribute—the daring vision to see my feet leaving the ground, the faith to imagine myself actually soaring through the air.

But my time on the track team wasn't wasted; oddly enough, while trying to figure out a way to take wing at the pole vault pit, I had a most grounding revelation about the intricacies of another track and field event: the relay race.

Relay races came in various lengths, but the one that interested me was the 4 x 400. Four separate sprinters would each run a one-hundred-and-ten-yard lap around the track, carrying a baton that they handed off to a teammate within a prescribed space at the end of their respective lap.

Although it sounded simple enough, it was anything but. Each of the four had to have distinct abilities and temperaments.

The first runner was called "the jackrabbit." He was the one quickest out of the blocks and thus most likely to get out in front of the pack, thereby establishing a lead. The second runner was almost as fast from the start but had to be able to exert more stamina in case he was required to make up any distance that the jackrabbit wasn't able to create; he was known as "the jet." The third runner was called "the mule." He was arguably the least skilled of the four. If the mule began his leg of the race in front, he was expected to maintain his position, if not lose too much of the lead he had been given. And if he began his lap chasing the leader, it was his responsibility to leave the final runner of the four at least within striking distance of the frontrunner.

The last sprinter was the star—"the rocket." He had to have the burst of the jackrabbit, the power of the jet, the steadiness of the mule, and the heart to make up for whatever shortcomings they each left him with.

What bound them all together was the baton; the entire spirit of the race was embodied in that hand-held cylinder. All of their effort and the seeming individuality of their energies was for nothing without that baton and its smooth hand-to-hand transmission.

Although there exists various schools of thought on how best to make the hand-off, the one our school team practiced was the most extraordinary. The runner awaiting the baton would stand in his lane, looking back to see his teammate approaching; and as that runner reached a certain marked place on the track, the awaiting teammate would begin running, his right hand extended backward, his fingers stretching mutely in a gesture of pure hope, determination, and anticipated acceptance.

As the back runner's rate declined slightly, he would slap the baton firmly into the lead runner's outstretched hand just as he was hitting his stride, enabling him to run blind because he had faith in his teammate to act, even if he couldn't see him or the baton he was passing. In doing so, they exhibited exactly the kind of vision about each other's abilities that I failed to manifest about my own.

Remembering the relay has helped me understand myself in a way that I hadn't considered in years. Like many of us, I grew up with a keen sense of my ancestors, something brought into even sharper focus by the Greek tradition of being named after my paternal grandfather.

There is something remarkable about sharing a name and heredity with someone you've never met, especially after that person has died. It feels as if something more than a name has passed; and as I ponder it, all I can see is the image of the baton. The object that binds you to people you may not even have known, but it's there, carried by one for a time, waiting to be handed to the next. And when you get it, it becomes part of you as you run your lap, and then you hand it off to be carried by another not unlike yourself.

In my case, though, there's a rub: I don't have a son to carry on the family name. I didn't even father a child to carry on our blood line. I am the last runner. Does that make me the rocket?

That question remains to be answered, as I'm still running my race, my baton firmly in hand. Unlike when I was young and couldn't envision being able to pole vault, I see the baton now. It's more than something just to be carried, though. It represents what I have learned and what I want to pass along. Knowing that there won't be any one specific person designated to hand it off to doesn't change that.

What it does do, though, is keep me open to finding someone who may or may not appear in my lane, their hand extended out, fingers splayed open, as they prepare to run their own race, which is definitely Greek to me.

The Last Cut is the Deepest

One of my life's greatest mysteries is how I rarely discover the value of an experience until long after it's over. For instance, when I worked in the steel mills to put myself through college, it was just a dirty means to a necessary end. It was years before I understood that watching steel actually being made from its rawest elements imbued me with an abiding curiosity and an essential need to question how something is created, and to study the forces that contribute to that result.

As with steel, so with Life's more esoteric commodities: custom, ritual, and especially tradition.

In the mid-1960s, barber shops were one of the last bastions of the male Old Guard. My dad's establishment, The Sportsmen's, was a rubicon of testosterone. Pictures of old fishing boats covered the walls. An ancient cash register chimed like a cathedral on Sunday morning whenever the cash drawer was opened. A seemingly endless supply of Doublemint gum occupied the slot where hundred-dollar bills would have gone, had any been exchanged.

But all of that was mere backdrop to the row of barber chairs that anchored the shop. They were lofty thrones in which leather, porcelain and metal merged in perfect harmony. To me, they were the eighth wonder of the world.

I remember as if it was yesterday the first time I ascended to my dad's chair. He had a special padded plank that stretched across its arms, so that even a speck of a boy my size could sit properly. Unknowingly, a tradition was born that day. When the haircut was over, my father splashed Old Spice on my face, plucked me out of the chair, threw me in the air, and kissed me roughly, the whiskers from his mustache prickling me with the most sublime fusion of pleasure and pain imaginable. This practice (and that sensation) was an augur of things to come. A time was dawning when how you wore your hair held political significance, and as that reality evolved, our relationship increasingly played out on what would become the battlefield of my scalp.

Pop's first volley in the Great Hair Wars involved crude chemical warfare. A strategic dab of ineffective Brylcreem led him to use an industrial-strength goop that was so densely unctuous he could have molded my hair into an octagon. I went to every extent imaginable to sabotage his efforts, which only brought out the tactician in him.

My father's response to my counter-offensive was a scorched earth policy he called "once around the block." It was a crew cut, which was devastating enough on its own. One summer, though, he sheared me on the day *before* school let out for the summer, knowing I would have to return to class for one last day and suffer needless ridicule in the process. From then on, the die was cast.

My tresses developed a mind of their own, coiling out in maddening loops. And even though Dad closed his shop, he continued to cut my hair. It was where we confronted each other within the confines of well-defined roles.

By high school, the warfare had taken on a guerrilla aspect. My hair hung over my eyes, shielding them from direct scrutiny. It flew unfettered, catching the wind, coming to rest wherever it fell. As a barber, Dad felt that my mop reflected poorly on him, professionally speaking. But, as a father, nothing irked him more personally.

Sitting for a haircut became hand-to-head combat. Though Pop was blessed with hands that could flutter above my head with nary a sound beyond the rhapsody of his scissors' serenade, when I was in his crosshairs, they became truncheons. And when I didn't sit properly, the metal comb he pulled through the thicket that sprang from my head became like an ancient plow dragged heavily across the crown of my skull by an aged farmer, busting old soil in an attempt to break new ground only he could see.

Matters reached a nadir when I came home from college one year with hair down to my shoulders; I was Medusa's twin brother, with snakes uncoiling every which way they could. Dad didn't so much surrender as just walk away in shear disgust. For a while there, an armistice was declared, and our tradition remained in abeyance.

A couple of years later we resumed our relative battle stations. My long hair was gone, but the scars of our fight were still fresh. One day as Pop was finishing me up, apropos of nothing and everything, I mused aloud that someday I should cut his hair. His scissors fell with a clatter—"That day will *never* come, son!"

Why is it that statements like that almost always dictate their opposite? That day came years later when Dad had fallen gravely ill, and I'd returned home to see him. He could no longer leave the house for any reason, least of all for something as seemingly inconsequential as a haircut.

But to Pop, it was anything but. With a look that conveyed some deep subterranean pain he couldn't name, he started muttering inaudibly. Finally, I heard him say that he needed to be "chopped up," which was his code for a haircut. Then Pop did the unthinkable—he asked me if I'd give him a trim. I froze for what felt like an eternity, and then agreed. *That day* had indeed arrived.

Life becomes time-lapse photography in moments like that. As I draped his favorite cape over his sagging shoulders, I felt a surreal sense of role-reversal. I felt this vertiginous clutch of literally not knowing what to do next. Instinctively, the actor in me took over, and I did the only thing I knew I could: I began aping the mannerisms and gestures I'd witnessed countless times over the years, all in an attempt to become him, if only for the next few minutes.

Miraculously, it worked. I lifted the wisps of his hair with the same metal comb he had used on me, clipping away at the limp strands pinched between my extended fingers, mimicking moves that left me feeling like a marionette being guided by a ghost I couldn't see as much as feel. Our exercise in mutual empathy ended when he asked me to trim his mustache. As the last snips ceased, I saw him gazing into the mirror. I imagined him to be entranced by the torrent of memories pouring off our reflection. Instead, he asked me a question I never saw coming:

"How'd you do it?"

Then, out of some celestial cellar I was unaware of, came…

"I watched you."

The words I spoke lanced the boil that had festered for all those years. When he stood up, he patted my face gently. Then he kissed me on the cheek, and all the childhood pain of his whiskers was gone.

A tradition did more than die that day: It left me with the realization that the best way to honor it is to participate in it fully while it's still vital, to let it go when it dies, and to have the wherewithal to create a new one when that happens.

Mercury Poisoning

When I was a kid, I accidentally broke a thermometer while at school. I watched the mercury spill out onto the desktop where I was sitting. Then, as the silver globules rolled to a halt, I tried picking them up, using my fingertips. They squished out from under my clumsy touch and skidded onto the floor. This scene repeated itself numerous times with increasing frenzy, as every blob that evaded my frustrated grasp split into numerous smaller versions of themselves. It wasn't long before I looked up to see my teacher watching me with what can only be described as a bemused gaze.

Unbeknownst to me, this was an introductory lesson in Life 101, entitled: Things That Look Really Easy But Aren't. And despite years of study and research, its message still confounds me today, especially as it relates to self-love.

But before I can even begin to address self-love, I have to speak to what I call "self-like." Do I regard myself as someone I enjoy and hold in high enough regard to potentially love? I'd hope to respond with an unqualified yes, but the plain and simple truth is this:

I'm just not that into me.

It seems to me that before you can truly like/love yourself, you have to know yourself. More than anything, I know that saying I'm a creature of habit would be like saying Jesus may have had a Messiah complex. And though that might be true, it doesn't keep me from liking him. Jesus' aforementioned flaw arguably only makes him more human and thus more compelling, while my routines feel like they alienate me from myself. Or at least from loving myself as fully as I might.

As for those habits, they span the gamut. From the behavioral (my mercurial temperament, my low tolerance for frustration), to the biological (my physical inability to sneeze gracefully), to the simply inane (for thirty-four years, the only cologne I ever wore was Old Spice).

So not only am I a slave to habit, I am judgmental about it, too. But wait a second—isn't love supposed to be unconditional? Aren't I supposed to love myself in spite of my flaws? Of course I am. And had I been conceived in a Petrie dish and then raised by wolves, I might be able to do so. But if there is one thing in life I have to get over if I'm ever going to be able to love myself, paradoxically, it is my self.

The earliest formulation of the self in modern psychology sprang from the distinction between the self as I, the subjective knower, and the self as Me, the object that is known. That's where a lot of my problems spring from: the relationship between my Subjective Knower and Me, the object that is supposed to be known. For reasons I still don't fully understand, I transactionally identify too closely with either one or the other persona, but rarely connect the two, leaving me in a state where I don't see myself clearly in either aspect.

It's a dilemma that was beautifully illustrated to me in one of my favorite movies, *Papillon.* In the movie, there's a scene in which Papillon, a charismatic career criminal, has been sentenced to solitary confinement on Devil's Island for his misdeeds. One day, just as he seems on the verge of death, he is called to his jail door for his routine inspection. Weakly poking his head through the small opening in his prison door, there, to his right, is another inmate, his head dangling limply from the hole in his door. Delirious and with one foot in the grave, amazingly, this wretch is even worse off than Papillon. When he sees Papillon, though, he gathers himself enough to ask him how he looks. In that instant, Papillon realizes that as bad as he has it, things could be worse—he could be *that* guy. In response to that realization, Papillon lies and tells the unfortunate convict that he looks fine, his words providing a temporary reprieve. The decrepit felon will live to see another day.

As I mentioned earlier, the scary thing is that I can identify with both men. All of which leaves me feeling remarkably like a kid who is still trying to grasp that which can't be held. But now, instead of it being some volatile element that skitters uncontrollably all around me, I'm coming to grips with the mercury that has coursed within my own veins, blinding me to the fact that while some things can never be fully grasped or comprehended, that awareness can't keep me from loving them.

And that self-love is much like any other form of love—it takes a leap of faith to achieve. The best I can do is love trying and hope I don't poison myself in the process.

Pelicans

oetry, I imagine, is one of those topics of interest I'll ultimately get to at some as-yet-undefined point in my life. I'll have ceased to live actively and withdrawn to a place where I engage in all those things I'll do when I'm too old to do anything else. In other words, it's a default choice.

When I mention this to my Uncle Tasso, I expect him to launch into an explanation of Aristotle's *Poetics* and the uses of speech in drama, comedy, rhetoric, and song. Instead, all I get is a reference to an old man from Nantucket with an affliction that really isn't one at all. Then, when I contemplate the added aspect of poetry as it relates to motion, I get brain-freeze—like I've just ingested too much intellectual ice cream and I'm left shivering, frigid, waiting for the thrumming numbness to subside.

Being blessed by living in close proximity to the ocean, I decide to go out for a walk. I venture out onto the pier that juts into the cove where I live. It's a weekday and the only other living being there is a brown pelican. Oddly enough, I've never seen one on the ground before. It has got to be one of the most ungainly creatures imaginable, looking like it stepped straight out of the pages of a Dr. Seuss book and into my life.

An impossibly narrow head droops into a rapier-like beak, sitting atop a neck that curls into an inverse question mark, which drains into an egg-shaped body standing on swizzle-stick legs attached to feet that look like they're dressed in avian Totes.

It is sitting on the rail, resting tranquilly, oblivious to me even when it's clear that I've gotten too close. Then it deigns to look at me as if to ask what I could possibly want. A mere stone's throw from a megalopolis of just under four million people, and this poor bird has the misfortune of getting stuck on a pier with a featherless interloper who wants a little quality face time.

Nuh-uh.

Then, out of nowhere, I experience one of those whipsaw interludes that takes a banal picture like that of a grounded pelican and inverts it with such alacrity and force as to jackhammer me into seeing the divinity of that image—the pelican has suddenly taken flight. And in so doing, he is transformed. His head and beak streamline seamlessly into his neck, melding into a body that has sprouted regal wings that carry him aloft with such grace that I expect to hear harps accompanying his elegant climb.

I watch him join a squadron of his peers. As they fly in perfect formation, flapping and coasting in unison, they become Mother Nature's answer to the Blue Angels, swooping and soaring with a precision that rivets me to the ground. Later that evening, I am lucky enough to witness them feeding—and it is then that the Blue Angels become kamikazes. They cruise over the ocean's surface, scouting for schools of fish; and when they spot one, dinner is served. One by one, they ascend perpendicular to the water, reach a lofty height, and then nosedive headlong into the sea. As I watch them, I think of that bird on the pier: then so ordinary, now, anything but.

∽

ON WEDNESDAY, APRIL 20, 2011, Tim Hetherington was killed by a rocket-propelled grenade in the besieged Libyan city of Misurata, when the rebel group he was with came under fire from pro-Qaddafi military forces. You may not know who Mr. Hetherington is; I first became aware of him after watching the Afghan war documentary, *Restrepo*. He directed and produced that film, a harrowing piece that chronicled the deployment of a platoon of American soldiers to one of the most dangerous locations in Afghanistan, the Korengal Valley. The soldiers' job was to build and maintain a fifteen-man outpost that was named after a platoon medic who was killed as they fought to secure the land the outpost stood on. Mr. Hetherington made it his job to document their efforts without outside commentary, so as to present war as it was lived by the soldiers—through their eyes and in their own words. It was an effort as heroic as that of its subjects.

He became what is known as "a conflict reporter," a photojournalist who embedded himself deeply within his subject in order to shed light on the darkest corners of the world. After reading of his tragic death, I saw a video clip of him discussing his work in war-torn Liberia.

Watching and listening, I was struck by how ordinary he seemed, almost common. This titan of bravery, compassion, and pro-activity reminded me of that pelican on the pier—absolutely unremarkable—that is, until he took flight. And when he did, I understood the poetry of motion—it is the animating force of an activity hurled at the person held in its thrall. Mr. Hetherington could no more refuse to go to places that chilled the blood than that pelican could refuse to dive for its sustenance—in each instance, it was what fed them, what nourished them. And in each example, the person who is lucky enough to witness the poet in motion is transformed, too.

By the time you read this, Mr. Hetherington's name will have in all likelihood faded from contemporary news. Hopefully, though, through his shimmering example, the poetry of his life will continue to soar long after the movement has ceased.

Tim Hetherington
December 5, 1970 – April 20, 2011

Walking (and Running) a Mile in Their Shoes

Where I grew up, local politics had all the sizzle of a rigged Yahtzee tournament. As a result, I couldn't imagine anything that could make political discourse seem even remotely interesting. Not even sex.

So, beyond voting, signing a few petitions, and writing the occasional e-mail to a congressman, I have no deep connection to politics. This is especially the case when it comes to that rarest animal of the political realm: sexual politics. If sexual politics is a war, I've always aspired to conscientious-objector status. If it's an election, I've abstained. But a couple of instances have made me realize that my position may not be as hermetically sealed as I'd like to believe.

I've served food for long enough to know that there are a few situations that you just don't want any part of. Like, never take sides in an argument that you may be privy to. Or, if anyone ever asks you to guess their age, never subtract more than ten percent of what you think they are, because it will be obvious that you're exaggerating. (Conversely, if someone ever asks you how they look, tell them, verbatim, "Like a million bucks in unmarked bills." It's corny but sounds flattering, and whatever its downside, by the time they figure that out, they'll be long gone.)

But there is one brick-wall quandary that isn't so readily solved, and I know this having run into it head-on at work recently.

My job is in a fine-dining establishment. It was a Sunday night, and business was even slower than usual. Now, Sunday night poses myriad problems if you happen to be working in a restaurant. In addition to being typically slow, business-wise, it's also renowned for being the night when the staff is most likely to be negligent because they've expended most of their energy and attention the night before. And the final reason that Sunday night can conjure the perfect storm is because it is the one night you're most likely to be visited by aliens—not extraterrestrials—but people who don't normally dine out. *Those* aliens.

I knew there was trouble the minute my manager approached me with hooded eyes and a hushed voice. He'd just personally seated a highly distraught customer in my section. It seemed, that though this person was clearly a man, he was dressed like a woman. He wore a wig that on its best day would have qualified for federal relief as an unnatural disaster. The floral print of his dress was so bright, it would have lent eyesight to a blind man, only to then blind him all over again. And the high heels he wore groaned pathetically under his considerable weight. (Think Dick Butkus in drag, but not as cuddly.)

What upset the guest so deeply was that, in the few minutes he had been in the restaurant, three employees had addressed him as if he were a man, despite his attire. It was now my mission to somehow undo the harm that had been inflicted. As the gravity of the situation quickly sank in, I resigned myself to living in a godless world.

Thus I froze, not knowing what my tack would be: Should I acknowledge the gaffes suffered, apologizing as a means of starting over? But just then I remembered something my dad had taught me when I was a young boy. He owned a beauty salon where many of his customers were extremely old to my eight-year-old eye, leaving me no way to relate to them beyond the obvious. Seeing my discomfort, Pop made a suggestion, but framed it as a game: Instead of seeing them as aged matrons, I was to treat them like young beauty queens, something I swallowed hook, line and wrinkle.

Repositioned, I now greeted the guest at my table warmly, without referring to gender in any way. She looked like a large wet bird whose feathers had been severely ruffled. Slowly, I massaged them back into place. I was attentive without stooping; and as I felt her relax, I began to play with her, essentially flirting without the sometimes requisite charge. Then she gestured me to come close. I was dreading the fatal, "Could you please direct me to the lady's room?" but as I leaned in, she asked me instead if there was a public phone available. Concealing my enormous sense of relief due to her benign inquiry, while instantly confirming the existence of a benevolent deity watching over us, I casually directed her to the back of the restaurant.

When it came time for her to leave, my beauty queen offered me her gloved hand. I did what I had to do, indeed, the only thing I could do—I kissed it, which seemed to wipe the slate clean. But as she turned to exit, one of her high heel's broke with a snap that smacked of nothing good, unceremoniously toppling her. She stopped as if she'd been shot, and immediately tried to jam the heel back into place. But it was no use. As she hobbled out the front door, my last image was of her struggling to regain the equipoise she had struck just a few minutes prior.

I WAS REMINDED OF HER recently when reading about Caster Semenya, the female South African runner who is the current world champion in the 800 meters. Ms. Semenya has become an inadvertent lightning rod because of the controversy surrounding her gender. In fact, ever since she qualified for the world championship last August, in Berlin, the issue of her biological validity as a woman has been batted back and forth between governments and sports federations alike. Winning the world championship in record time only threw gas onto a fire that had established its own manic blaze.

Her case and the firestorm that it has spawned have engulfed science, sports, politics and ethics, stirring them all together inside a most unlikely bubbling cauldron. As was pointed out in an exhaustive piece on this topic by Ariel Levy, in the November 30, 2009, issue of *The New Yorker*, "The only thing more slippery than the science in the Semenya case is the agendas of the men who have involved themselves in it. There is a bounty of political gain for whomever spins the story most successfully."

What struck me about both people I've mentioned

here is that each one of them wanted nothing more than to walk (or run) in the shoes that they felt fit them best. One example was microcosmic, the other macrocosmic. But underlying both is a core need to be precisely who they are, independent of what others see, expect, or desire of them.

To me, those are eminently reasonable expectations. And if we can't extend ourselves to others by perhaps trying on their shoes, metaphorically speaking, then the only option left for us is easy:

To walk away.

Paradise Lost and Found: My Homeric Summer

I grew up in a family that was so close-knit we had our own mutant Theory of Relativity: It stated that no one could go anywhere without the other four. Obviously, this limited my own personal movement, and for the first eighteen years of my life, the farthest I was able to get away from my home was when I went on vacation with my family (of course) to some ramshackle cottages a mere hour-and-a-half from where we lived. And though our time spent there was remarkable in its own right, it cemented the notion that I was rooted to a place with no prospects for escape, temporary or otherwise.

I finally decided that had to change. So, the summer after I graduated from high school, I figured I would journey to Greece to walk the land where my ancestors trod, while connecting with my ancient Greek forebear Homer—epic poet and author of *The Odyssey*. (Oh, I should mention that my "odyssey" was going to include a traveling companion in the form of a beautiful, blonde classmate whose golden mane smelled of Flex shampoo and promise.)

When I told my father of my plan, he was unmoved,

asking how I was going to fund my sojourn. When I expressed the hope that he might be of some help, an all-knowing smile crept across his face. Heartfelt and swift, he assured me of his assistance. The following week he "helped" me, alright—by securing me a job fixing flat tires on the city of Hammond's garbage trucks.

As one odyssey died, another was born.

That first morning my mom dropped me off on her way to work, leaving me standing outside the bunker that was the municipal garage where I would be toiling for the next three months. As I approached the large metal door, it opened from above as if it were an ancient dragon preparing to devour me whole.

Entering the garage's maw, I was assaulted by the smells that lived there. A dizzying swirl of sweat, grease and men. Then, against the far wall, I saw them clumped together; a writhing, roiling, radioactive mound of masculine energy, each form blurring into the next.

Just then, a tall black shadow of a man descended from a catwalk high above the garage floor. Coincidentally, his name was Homer, and, though no epic poet, he identified himself as the foreman. In a sonorous voice, he announced, "Everybody, this is Michael. He's going to fix flat tires. Show him around." And with that, he retreated to his office.

The first member of the scrum to address me directly was a guy old enough to be my grandfather. His name was Freddie, and his grimy glasses perched on a nose so red it almost looked fake. At the time, I wore colorful glass beads on a choker around my neck. When Freddie saw the beads, he mockingly pointed at them, crudely questioning my sexual orientation.

It was going to be a long, hot summer.

But I made peace with Freddie by dropping him off at his favorite tavern while we made our appointed rounds. He'd get his "liquid breakfast" while I continued working. I'd pick him up on my return to the garage, his crimson snout even redder than when I left him.

Freddie was just one of many men I'd get to know that summer. Over my first few days in the garage, my eyes learned to adjust to the garage's dark shadows, enabling me to discern separate beings amid the raging sea of testosterone, even if I didn't know their names.

There was a solidly built older Black man with just one arm that appeared so strong that it looked like someone had sown a leg onto his torso. There was another man who seemed as big as a mountain—that is, until his work partner stood next to him, when he dissolved into an outsized foothill. The two youngest of the crew were the funniest to watch: one was a slight-framed fella with a slight hunch on the left side of his back, behind his shoulder. His partner was in his mid-twenties and possessed a shock of dirty blond hair that completely obscured his eyes, which was probably for the better because, despite his youth, he wore glasses so thick he looked pop-eyed. They formed a two-man team of street sweepers who walked all over the city, pushing a cart that held nothing more than a garbage can, with a few brooms and rakes propped atop it, looking as if they'd stepped out of a Rocky and Bullwinkle cartoon.

Not surprisingly, my favorite co-worker was the first to introduce himself to me—Jimmy the Preacher. He was like some aged lightning bolt housed in a compact body, taut as piano wire. The Preacher often took refuge on the roof of the garage, where he'd play a knife game called mumblety-peg: He'd splay his pristine fingers on a chunk of gnarled tree stump, spearing the wood between them with staccato thrusts of his glistening blade. Fortunately, his aim was always perfect.

As the blistering summer wore on, each day melted into the next, and I came to understand the rhythm of the garage. And by submitting to it, I became adept at tasks for which I'd never exhibited any facility. I made the unthinkable transition from being all thumbs to actually becoming handy. Most important, though, I learned that the best way to get along with my co-workers was by pulling my weight.

In fact, I got along well with everyone except one of the garbage men who inexplicably hated me. He'd drift in and out of my work space, following me around the garage, cursing me. Naturally, I avoided him. But, one day, late in the summer, he cornered me. Desperate, I retreated to the rooftop where I knew The Preacher was hiding out, crouched on a stool. Seeing Jimmy, my nemesis shifted his focus. He stood over Jimmy and taunted him for being an old man. The Preacher seemed oblivious, which only fueled more violent threats.

Suddenly, out of nowhere, Jimmy levitated off his stool, his switchblade materializing at his foe's throat. It turned out the Preacher was a master knife-fighter, storing his blade in his boot. As I saw his extended arms, I noticed a lattice of scars that criss-crossed them—mementos of past clashes. The knife's point poked a hole in the bully's bloated ego as he evaporated into thin air.

On my last day, as I waited on the garage floor for my paycheck, I looked around. What had started out as a faceless, shapeless gang had become a working-class Periodic Table of Elements whose chemistry was a privilege to work within: One Pound, Little Ronnie, Big Ronnie, Polish Chester, Blind Tony and the Flying Hunch, diamonds in the rough, forged in the kiln of thankless manual labor.

As Homer descended from the catwalk, he called for everyone's attention. Homer being a man of few words, the crew took note. As we all gathered around, Homer suddenly turned to me, addressing me directly. He told me that when I started no one thought I'd last the week. But not only did I last, Homer said, I'd worked as hard as everyone else. So, unbeknownst to me, the crew had asked Homer to lobby his bosses for a pay-raise on my last check, so that I was paid commensurate with what everyone else made.

As he shook my hand, Homer said, "Take this check. Remember your work here and be proud." He paused for a second, almost as if to leave. Then, out of nowhere, he spoke words that hit me like a wrecking ball. "And don't ever come back—you have better things to do."

By going to Greece I'd hoped to experience life in grand proportion, in realms I'd never seen before. Working in the garage that summer, I'd done just that. But Homer's words still resound to this day, as I ask myself whether I've met the standard of getting better things done.

Being here, on this page, I think is a step that both Homers would have appreciated.

Winter

A Tree Has Fallen: A Eulogy in Three Acts

Growing up in the 1960s, freedom was a national obsession, the province of the young. My initial vision of it was to be liberated from the constraints imposed by family and society, to be free to be me, whoever that was. Like all things, though, freedom has its price, and I found myself asking what it would mean to gain my freedom if something had to die.

My father has been a constant source of friction in my life. That isn't nearly as negative as it sounds. You see, I need friction. I've understood this concept ever since I was a kid and saw an episode of *Wild Kingdom* in which I learned that young caribou need trees to rub their budding antlers against. It strips them of the fuzzy felt in which they're coated—a vital step in the animal's development. Unconsciously, my father was my tree of choice, the one I most often scraped my antlers against, long past the time the fuzz had been knocked off.

ACT I

In late spring of 2007, I made a trip home to northwest Indiana. My mom was scheduled to have surgery, and her failing health captured my family's attention. My mission was to ferry my father into Chicago every day to see my mother. Those trips became sprawling episodes in which we interacted like renegade bumper cars trapped in a joyless carnival.

Through it all hung a Damoclean sword, never referred to, always at play. With each passing day the thread that held the sword aloft frayed. And with each passing mile the air inside the car grew thick with a deadening tension. It was a situation brought to a nuclear head when the highway we were on was closed due to an accident. We were rerouted to a surface road that abutted a steel mill, requiring us to cross a drawbridge. As we approached it, the bridge was raised to allow a hulking ship to pass beneath it—we were now literally facing a wall, staring directly at the street that seconds before was going to be beneath us, with nowhere to go.

The depth of our predicament finally moved my father to broach a topic whose familiarity was out-stripped only by its volatility: our relationship. With surgical precision, he recounted a phone conversation we'd had years earlier, one in which I'd confessed to a loneliness that was so deep I literally ached. Sometime during that exchange on the phone, I cried. As I drove, Dad asked me whether I knew how it felt for him to hear me in that state—a grown man, educated and strong, reduced to blubbering to his dutiful father about being lonely. Perplexed, I admitted I'd never considered it. That's when my father told me that for all the work and sacrifice he'd made in order to guarantee my success, I was an abject failure. A fuck-up.

The sword fell, impaling me in time.

ACT II

A year passed. I didn't return home. Whenever I got my dad on the phone, our prior discussion was never mentioned. Now it was me who was dangling by a thread, twisting with no direction, waiting to fall. Then one afternoon I called to check in and instantly heard it in his voice—he was dying—and I landed with a thud.

ACT III

A red-eye flight got me back to Indiana in time to see the morning sun open its veins, staining the sky crimson: blood was in the air. That which binds one man to another drenched me. I was racked with fear at the prospect of confronting the looming sequoia I perceived my father to be, and all I prayed for was to be love—to embody it in whatever form it took because I'd been bled dry and it was all I had left.

I saw my father that morning; the towering tree had been reduced to a desiccated trunk. There was no light in his eyes, only resignation. I wanted to cry but I remembered his words of a year ago, so I dammed the brine that rushed my eyes. Then, all I wanted was to be love, and love showed up dressed as faith.

I knelt down in front of him, extending my arms. He rested his head on my chest. We began a week-long dance during which I became his bulwark. Because he was so weak, I cleaned him, I fed him. At night when he tried to sleep, he rang a bell to let me know when he needed something. Love appeared as the strength to go without sleep, while performing tasks of previously unthinkable intimacy.

Finally, love showed itself in its grandest expression of all: surrender.

As I stooped to raise him, Dad put his hands on my shoulders, assessing me. He commented that I'd kept in shape, something that he respected. Then, seemingly out of nowhere, he told me that I was a beautiful man. Caught off-guard, I reflexively batted his compliment down, and responded that whatever I was, I owed to him. But as he repeated himself, the words I'm sure he meant as praise instead lodged in my flesh like rusty harpoons that I'd carried in pained silence since our talk the previous year. And all I could do was look him straight in the eye and tell him that whatever I was, I was not a fuck-up. I was not the man he accused me of being the year before, the words seeping from me as if I had lanced an unhealed scar…

My father then confessed that he'd been wrong, that I was indeed a beautiful man. As he rested his head on my shoulder, our tears cleansed our wounds, creating an opportunity to do something unprecedented—love each other unconditionally.

That exchange moved Dad to admit that he had no fight left in him to live. It reminded me of the admission I'd made years earlier about being lonely. But that was incidental to the real problem—Pop didn't know how to let go. Not knowing what to say, wanting just to be love, I opened my mouth and heard words that I had no cognitive awareness of but that were being spoken through me. I heard me tell him that it was all right to let go, that he was loved, and that we would all be okay.

He looked away, pondering the unthinkable and what I'd just shared. The man who'd spent his entire life holding on didn't know how to release life. Then he asked when I was returning to Los Angeles. When I told him, he requested I stay a couple of extra days. When I arranged for the extra time, he was grateful. He then asked when I was departing, specifically. When I told him, he said, "When you leave, I'm going, too."

EPILOGUE

Dad died sixteen days after I left. When he told me that he was going to depart when I did, I clutched for a moment. "Don't go on my account," I joked, only to be met by a look that instantly reminded me of our recent understanding, a pact from which we both unknowingly derived a great deal.

What freed me to leave him when I did was that I'd gained an authority I didn't previously have: to live my life knowing that the man who raised me had finally endorsed me in a way he couldn't before. And Pop acquired the power to ultimately let go of this life.

My father was the preeminent tree in the forest of my life. I was privileged to grow up in his loving shade. Like every tree when it falls, his memory feeds the ground where it landed, enriching the soil for generations to come.

From Dad I've learned the immutable lessons a tree imparts: the value of roots, the benefit of extending out to others, and the bliss that is ours merely by taking a moment to feel the wind blowing through our own branches.

Lastly, I've come to understand that we are all trees, capable of giving off benevolent shade or casting dark shadows. The choice is ours.

So when a tree falls, it doesn't matter if there is anyone there to hear the sound or not. What matters is that we acknowledge the loss, going forward with what it has taught us, even when all we can see and feel is the unavoidable fact:

A tree has fallen.

George Michael Raysses
July 31, 1927 – June 6, 2008

Shades of Gray

Thank God Leo Tolstoy had a sense of foresight that bears dividends even until this day. Beyond penning what many consider one of the best novels ever written, he presented us with a timeless theme—War and Peace. (Personally speaking, I'm just glad he opted out of writing a sequel entitled "Death and Taxes." But I digress…)

War and peace. I don't think it's any coincidence that you rarely, if ever, hear that phrase sequenced to read "peace and war." War is sexy. It commands top billing. Besides, war begets peace. Peace couldn't exist without war, right? It is war's logical conclusion. At least, that is what the proponents of war might have you believe.

We have recklessly lived and needlessly died as if war and peace are black and white, absolutes that exist in part only to define the other. We have romanticized and glamorized war. Peace, on the other hand, gets the kind of lip service typically reserved for eating one's vegetables and watching PBS: healthy and edifying, with absolutely nothing to elicit passion beyond practical utility.

War, with its inherent blackness, has been painted onto our cultural canvas as artfully as a grand master blends dissonant hues to create a seemingly harmonized whole, blotting out whatever light peace may have brought to the picture. And it has done so at our peril.

War seduces us with lies about its illusory necessity and its false value. It taps into our primal need to marshal ourselves as individuals into groups that represent ideals that are worth battling and killing for. It also poses the impossibly alluring prospect of ennobling lives by the mere fact of one gesture—the willingness to fight. To wage war. And in so doing, to confer heroism on what might otherwise be a meaningless, if not dull, life. Ironically, by making the ultimate sacrifice by dying in the service of that act, a perverse sense of immortality can be achieved.

Bullshit.

Before you dismiss this as so much liberal cant, ask yourself this: why do we name wars as we do? It's not as if they are going to be confused with one another. It's because we value them as watershed events that define us. Beyond that, look at the names we choose to bestow on these tragedies: The Great War. The War to End All Wars. And in one of this country's greatest acts of self-deception and self-loathing, the Civil War—a conflict named to capture the sheer lunacy of citizens killing citizens in a conflagration that ultimately came to represent savagery and carnage that is remarkable even by today's jaded standards. (And don't even get me started on how history will label the debacle that took place in Iraq in the early 2000s—The Grand Clusterfuck would not be inaccurate in my mind. Besides, I love understatement.)

Yet we never give a name to those times in which we aren't actively engaged in warfare with someone else.

(And no, "peacetime" counts only as dismissive cultural lip service—sorry.) The absence of war is simply known as peacetime, a brief recess, a destination to be glided over while en route to someplace else. Someplace that inevitably leads back to war.

What brings all of this into focus for me is how the very aspects of our society that I am decrying play out in my own life. I will suffer some personal setback, which then becomes a problem. I let the problem fester until it reaches critical mass. Now things have reached a crisis state—and my solution?

To declare my own personal war.

I take on an embattled demeanor, as I set my jaw and narrow my gaze. All my attention is riveted on that issue. Now I am thoroughly engaged. I feel alive as I plan my attack. It's a feeling that is heightened as I execute my plan, and even as I feel the inevitable ebb and flow that comes with solving the riddles of one's own life, I hum with the electric thrum required of me in this time and place. In that moment when I conquer my enemy, there is nothing but celebration.

Afterwards, there is, once again, the absence of war. But there's no real peace because true serenity isn't a destination—it is an elusive state of being. It is a calm reached by reconciling the impulse to reflexively wage war with the delusion that war's absence is peace.

It is striking an ineffably intricate balance by having the courage to make sense of that which exists between war's pitch black and the luminous white of true peace—the ever-shifting continuum of the inscrutable shades of gray that *make up our lives.*

Until we address those seemingly vague and varied

tones while learning to live with them in a spirit of genuine tranquility, we are consigned to swinging helplessly between black and white, pendulums with no sense of purpose beyond the irresistible force of our own momentum.

And the greatest casualty won't be the war that we didn't win but the peace that we lost.

Killing Time and Other Small Crimes

I don't know much. I really don't. One of the things I'm learning, though, is that if I'm to have any chance of success in any sense of the word, I need lists. Lists of things to do, because, if left to my own devices, I will drift so egregiously as to get nothing done. Thus, my dependence. Hell, writing this essay is on my list, okay?

On my Existential To-Do list, however, I set out those things that I want to accomplish before I die. Right behind Numbers One (grow more hair) and Two (off-handedly use the word "crepuscular" while chatting with a beautiful linguist) is something that weighs heavily on me of late: reconcile my life with Time.

Time? Yeah, Father Time. You know—the guy with the hourglass and the scythe. He looks good in black, that guy. We've had a tortured relationship, he and I. One that has lured me into a life of unwitting criminality.

Though I don't recall exactly when we met, I do remember being faintly aware of him when I was young. He was elusive and hard to define. For instance, when I was unable to sleep on Christmas Eve while waiting for the morning to come, Time was there, sitting at the foot of my bed, refusing to budge. Minutes felt like days. And there was that one Fourth of July when I asked my mom how long it would be before I had to go back to school. "Oh, honey," she replied, "you're only halfway through the summer." And Time stretched out languidly, seeming infinite.

My sharpest recollection of Time, though, was when I was five years old and I asked my dad how long it would be before I was seven: two years may as well have been eternity.

Gradually, though, we developed a decent working relationship, Time and me. The years would come and go in a rhythm that became familiar and well within my grasp. And even in those moments when I sensed him becoming a tad slippery, loosening what I believed was my grip on him, we ultimately fell back into a routine that felt right. Unbeknownst to me, this ultimately suited Time much more than it did me.

You see, Time holds the copyright on routine. And anytime you fall into one, you pay him a royalty. A fee fashioned from a little piece of your heart. And if you think you're exempt from the "routine tax" because you're chasing a dream, think again.

When I turned 27, I quit being a lawyer to become an artist. I was going to act, maybe even write a little. I was home visiting my parents; when I told my dad my plan, he gave me a fatherly heads-up. Resigned to my choice, he cautioned me, "Just be careful of time. You have less than you think."

Driving home that night, I scoffed at Pop's advice— what did Time have on me? I had nothing but time. And besides, I was young and armed with arrows dipped in the elixir of my dreams. Time posed no threat to me. In fact, I was going to have my way with Time by taking mine. It was, quite literally, *my* time to take.

So I proceeded to spit in Time's eye. I ignored him. I refused to acknowledge him. I never wore a watch, and wouldn't consult a calendar to save my life. I spent time like a kid in a candy store spends money. Even worse, I got good at wasting it, mangling it, and ultimately committing a capital offense against it—killing it. And even in those moments when I felt hung over from my own drunken belligerence to him, I maintained my defiant posture.

That is, until that first time when a year passed so quickly that I felt like someone had picked my soul's pocket—I was 35 years old.

It was early January, I was living in Los Angeles. I was at the bank, standing at the teller's window, writing a check, thinking I'd made the adjustment for the changing new year, when she pointed out that I hadn't. Wait a second, I thought—that was a year? All I remembered were the holidays, my mom's birthday, and a brief stop at Thanksgiving—where did Time go?

Had I not been blinded by his brilliant deception, I would have seen him standing there, not looking nearly as feeble as I might've hoped. It turns out Time loves Los Angeles. In Los Angeles there are no seasons, no telltale signs to mark his passage. (There's a joke out here that says when you move to L.A. you find an apartment, you go down to the pool, and by the time you get back to your apartment, ten years have passed. It would be funny if it weren't so true.)

As I write these words I'm 50, and I struggle mightily to reverse the error of my ways. But it's a rigged match—

Time marches on. Time bats last. There is no negotiating with him.

The one and only thing that slows Time down for me, though, is writing—the act of trying to bottle the lightning that lit me up oh so many years ago by chaining thoughts and feelings to words.

There's an irony here that isn't lost on me—that now I stand accused of attempting to steal back time. And as I await the punishment for my crimes, I hear my sentence:

"Life. *My* life."

Timely, wouldn't you say?

Consider the Writer

"An ad that pretends to be art is—at absolute best—like somebody who smiles warmly at you only because he wants something from you. This is dishonest, but what's sinister is the cumulative effect that such dishonesty has on us: since it offers a perfect facsimile or simulacrum of goodwill without goodwill's real spirit, it messes with our heads and eventually starts upping our defenses even in cases of genuine smiles and real art and true goodwill. It makes us feel confused and lonely and impotent and angry and scared. It causes despair."
—*from "A Supposedly Fun Thing I'll Never Do Again" by David Foster Wallace*

desperado: (n.) a reckless or desperate person, esp. one ready to commit any violent illegal act.

Around the time of my last birthday, my wife Jill had a present neatly wrapped and ready, well in advance of the actual date. It was obviously a book; heavy and thick, it begged to be identified before a shred of wrapping paper had been removed. I hoisted it to see if its weight would somehow reveal its identity, to some avail. As I half-expectantly ripped the paper back I saw the word "Jest," and I immediately knew it was David Foster Wallace's magnum opus, *Infinite Jest*.

Hmm.

To modern fiction, this is arguably Moby Dick, the whale, not the book, reborn as a novel. More than any tome published in the last 15 years, it created a wake so gaping that most people I knew who ventured into its froth and foam did so in groups, a tacit admission that to go it alone was to risk being lost at sea.

Even a guy like me who wasn't immersed in fiction was aware of it and its singular impact. It was a one-thousand-and-seventy-nine-page literary leviathan that showcased Wallace's range of prowess and depth of focus; all predicated on an intellect that was leavened with low-brow grenade-lobs of humor and wit that had the incongruous effect of making his prose that much more consequential and sinewy.

As appropriate a gift as the book seemed, there was an element to it that was problematic—sooner or later I would have to sit down and scale this monolith, a feat that I would put right up there with running a marathon or climbing a mountain. But that was only half the problem; the other half being that I am one of those writers who, whatever I'm reading, if it's well done, I think should be writing my own version of it.

(Who put the "fun" in dysfunction? That would be me.)

So, in a low-level run-up to possibly committing to reading it, I researched Mr. Wallace. Novelist, essayist, journalist, he wrote in all manner of format and genre, losing none of his trademark glint and verve in the process. *Infinite Jest* was just his second novel. And if you were making a movie about a contemporary writer who you not only loved to read but who you rooted for as a person, David Foster Wallace would be that writer.

Growing up in the Midwest, he came from an educated, middle-class family. He was self-effacing and charismatic, with a shambling way of speaking that brimmed with spark and promise. And if all that weren't enough to make you want to sing his praises as a most extraordinary ordinary man, he suffered from something that acutely humanized him: depression.

So much so, that on September 12, 2008, after a lengthy bout of despair in which all of the various treatments that had worked previously failed him, he hanged himself on the patio of the home that he shared with his wife and two dogs.

Knowing that Mr. Wallace died at his own hand made me want to understand why he wrote *Infinite Jest*. It was an inquiry that shed much light. "Fiction's about what it is to be a fucking human being," he once observed, and that good writing should help readers to "become less alone inside."

Specifically, with this book, Mr. Wallace wanted to address the pain that he saw in so many of his contemporaries, an affliction not of circumstance but one so fundamental as to be cellularly visceral. This would be a lofty goal under any scenario, but as the object of a piece of fiction, it approached the sublimely impossible. A fool's task actually worth aspiring to.

I think about his example when I write, not because I merit being mentioned in the same sentence as him, but because I think of the things I share with him when he wrote: For me, I think of my desire to somehow make things better for the person willing to partner with me by reading what I'm offering. I think about the war that is declared when a writer decides he has to write something specific as a matter of life and death.

And I think about the enemy in that fight, the blank page. Because the minute a writer articulates what he wants to say, every blank page becomes a battle ground. From that moment forward, the void of the blank page taunts him, because in his mind's eye he sees it filled, overrun with the word-soldiers he's dispatched to carry his message, whatever it may be, to whomever shows up to read it.

But if the author fails in his mission, if he can't muster the troops, the blank page defiantly stares back. It is no different than the moment it was created. And the writer? He dangles and twists in the wind of his own fevered realization that he's been bested by a cypher that barely registers the faint shadow of the author's unmet, unrealized expectation. And, for me, that is as bad as it gets. It sometimes makes me desperate because it's hard to live knowing that out there somewhere is a blank page waiting for me, one whose emptiness will fill me.

Whether you write or not, we all have our version of the blank page. David Foster Wallace literally stared down one-thousand-seventy-nine of his when he wrote *Infinite Jest*. It was a fully realized attempt that reflected the life and death stakes that writing imposed on him, with death tragically having the last word.

Hunting: A Day in the Life

Peple often comment that they're "getting back to nature" but I find that whole concept to be a banana peel, strategically positioned to invite a slip-and-fall of indeterminate outcome. The very essence of that phrase implies my having been there in the first place (I wasn't). And if the Bible is any authority in this regard (it's not), we've arguably been trying to get back to nature ever since Adam and Eve got their divine eviction notice.

But if I am required to turn to nature, the vehicle that gets me there is my memory—that rusting clunker that I garage somewhere in the expanse between my head and heart. The one whose crank I turn with increasing frequency if only because I'm all too aware of the gap between what the number on the odometer conveys versus how I feel.

I take it out for regular spins. Sometimes the ride is a sprint, in which speed is as important as the endpoint. Other times the trip is a marathon, and I've forgotten how to get where I want to go. This is where my memory defies logic because, unlike every other vehicle I've known, *it* drives *me,* picking me up based on the subtlest of triggers: a meandering smell wafting through the air, a random sound, a fleeting image so scant that it skims my subconscious, barely felt.

I was recently taken back by a song I'd heard hundreds of times before, the Beatles' *A Day in the Life*. This time, though, for some unknown reason, it transported me to when I was barely old enough to begin thinking about who I was beyond my name and my status as a member of my family.

I was nine or so, and resigned to the notion that I was never going to be a Beatle, something I had devoted a lot of energy to up until that point in time. Even with that realization, though, I still tried to pass myself off as a friend of the Fab Four by blackening the back side of a Beatles card and claiming it was a Polaroid picture I'd taken at a concert they'd given at a local country club. Or there was the time I called Ronnie Whitfield on the telephone and told him that the Beatles were at my house playing for me, my proof being the scratchy 45 I played in the background. But Ronnie was too cagey to fall for my radioactive fantasy. Not becoming a Beatle cast me adrift—who was I? What was I? Most important, what was *my nature?*

Enter my dad and his older brother, John.

They were hunters. Which is to say, every autumn they would pull out their shotguns, donning long underwear and hats I couldn't imagine wearing anyplace but where you were highly unlikely to see anyone else—or at least anyone who wasn't also wearing a likeminded brim. They would find some distant patch of land on the farthest reaches of some unknown farm, and traipse through fields in search of game—"game" being rabbits or pheasants or ducks. Each species had its own season, some of which overlapped, something I found odd because I thought that each animal somehow knew when it was its respective season and dreaded it accordingly.

Looking back, they probably hunted for a couple of reasons. Practically speaking, we actually ate whatever they bagged. It was also a chance for them to maintain a brotherly connection. And just maybe it provided them an opportunity to get back to nature—by tromping around and shooting off firearms whose percussive bangs punctured the silence typically found on a farm very early in the morning. Or as my Uncle John so eloquently put it, by "busting geese."

Regardless of why, hunting was a big deal for all involved. It required getting up so early that it was still dark, something that would never have occurred to me. It felt like some bad practical joke we were playing on the sun by beating it to its appointed rounds. Over time, though, I understood it as part of a special project undertaken only by men, which ultimately struck me as something cool if only because it began to fill in the blank that was me.

After bundling ourselves against the cold and filling thermoses full of steaming coffee, we'd drive silently into the inkwell countryside. Once there, guns were loaded with great deliberation and a hushed calm draped the ritual in ceremony. Although it was technically still dark as we stood around our car, off to the east I could almost hear the sky release its fierce grip on the night so gradually, as if it were laying down a precious item it could no longer bear to hold but didn't want to break.

Eventually, my dad and uncle spoke, though in a stage whisper: loud enough to be heard, but their words delivered in such a way that great effort was expended to respect the quiet, despite the sound. I took my cue from them. Not talking reduced me to spectating. Everything seemed new, freshly minted. The dew on the ground reminded me of floor wax, making the ground shiny and slippery.

Guns ready, we set out. Sometimes we'd walk in fields, down rows of corn that had long since been harvested, the fallen stalks crisscrossing the ground. My feet would get tangled and I'd fall like the corn, something that felt as unmanly a thing as I could do.

Initially, my job was to keep pace and not fall behind. But by my third time out, I was tasked with wearing the game coat: a jacket with large pockets inside it to store our take. Once we were walking between a railroad track and a creek when we spooked a rabbit ahead of us. Uncle John dispatched it with a shot, grabbing its limp body and dropping it into the game coat, right next to the pocket closest to my chest. No sooner was the flap closed than I felt this frantic thumping where the rabbit was—it'd come back to life and was thrashing mightily, trying to get out! I was so shocked I couldn't even scream. I stood riveted to the ground, mutely waving my arms as if trying to take flight. In motion as fluid as the rabbit's was frantic, my uncle reached in, pulled it out by its ears, gave it a swift chop to the back of its neck, and dropped it back into the pocket where it'd been an instant earlier.

I'll never forget that feeling; what had been so alive a second before was now a leaden bag of fur and bone, literally dead weight, its fading warmth now pressing against my body.

I think of that incident almost every time I hear *A Day in the Life*. In that song's famous final chords, a musical technique called deceptive cadence was used, whereby the listener assumes the next chord or melody note will go somewhere it doesn't. We're led to expect a certain outcome, but the writer/arranger intentionally surprises us by musically going someplace else.

Like that song's interminable last chord, my hunting experience led me to expect a certain outcome, but I ended up some place else altogether. I was trying to take a step toward becoming what I thought was a man, only to discover that path is defined by its missteps as much as by its forward progress.

Leaving me with the game, the prize, that says: sometimes when you go hunting for one thing, you end up inadvertently bagging another—which is lyrically Greek to me.

Cross My Heart

There are many transitions to be negotiated if you're lucky enough to burrow your way into middle age. I surrendered the obvious big issues early on. For instance, I've long since given up trying to be actively cool in favor of not making a fool of myself. And I don't even feign knowing who the latest hot actors and musicians are, something that happened around the time I pronounced "Beyonce" so that it rhymed with "séance."

But I still envision being sharp. You know—smart. So, I would like to tell you that when I sat down to write this piece, I seized on an approach that involved nineteenth-century French art and literature, but I didn't. Instead, I came up with *Ben Casey*, which was a 1960s TV show whose opening titles consisted of a lone hand drawing the symbols for man, woman, birth, death, and infinity on a chalkboard, while a voice intoned as much.

The symbols foreshadowed the show's ambit, which was how I became a huge fan of symbols. They did the heavy lifting. Which only led me to appreciate phrases and gestures that pack symbolic meaning. And the one I most readily embraced was when I crossed my heart after speaking, to signify that I had just told an unimpeachable truth. It was a gesture that came to be embodied in a gold cross that I wore around my neck.

The cross was a gift from my mother. It's an amalgam of the Greek letters alpha and omega, interwoven with the Orthodox cross itself. Symbolically, the alpha represents the beginning, the omega represents the end, and the cross everything in between.

My love for it was heightened because it hung from a chain given to me by a dear childhood friend. It was masculine yet ornate. When my mother gifted me the cross, it and the chain and I all merged. And I found it only fitting that as the cross hung from the chain, it rested directly over my heart.

Beyond its beauty, though, I embraced it because it represented things I believed in: family, friends, and a Higher Power. Which was all well and good. That is, until I had occasion to see it in a new light.

MANY YEARS AGO, REILLY, an actor friend of mine from Chicago, was in town filming a movie. He called me from his hotel to join him for dinner. While we were there, his phone rang—the caller was Sean Penn, who had called to invite him to dinner. (Having just worked with Reilly on a film, Penn would become instrumental in helping him get established as an actor.) Reilly hung up, and told me we were now both going out to dinner with Penn.

We met at a famous Hollywood eatery. Reilly and I arrived early, initially getting Los Angeles' version of the

Bum's Rush—a social loop-de-loop in which someone ignores you by looking right through you. However, that changed the instant Penn arrived. As if by magic, we were escorted to the best table in the restaurant. The same people who did barrel rolls to avoid Reilly and me now hovered like hummingbirds to attend our every need. This was my first tutorial in Hollywood's social algebra: a non-celebrity + a celebrity = a Celebrity by Association. Reilly and I were special now, too.

Later, we adjourned to Penn's favorite watering hole, where a torrent of dignitaries all stopped by to greet him. It was surreal: cultural icons, sports figures, and artists of various levels of accomplishment, all paraded by us to chat with Penn.

Now, up to that point, Penn and Reilly had done most of the talking. I was content just taking things in. That changed, though, when Penn told a story in which he'd gotten into a high-speed chase involving the police. When the cops finally apprehended him, Penn said, they treated him brusquely, which shocked him. Incredulous, I asked him what did he expect?

Penn looked stunned. I had friends who were cops, and they told me that the hardest part of a high-speed chase was when the pursuit was finally over. Confronting the perpetrator was frightening because the cops didn't know who they were going to have to deal with.

Surprisingly, when I explained this to Penn, he understood. From that point on, he opened up to me a lot more. So much so, that later in the wee hours of the morning when we parted ways, he invited me back to the bar to join him anytime I was in the neighborhood. I assured him that I'd return.

The next morning when Reilly and I were having breakfast, he asked me if I was going to reconnect with Penn any time soon. Without a moment's hesitation, I said no. When he asked why, I reminded him that I was from Gary, Indiana—what could I possibly have in common with Sean Penn? Bewildered, Reilly shook his head and said nothing more.

The years passed and Reilly's star ascended; he became John C. Reilly, a fully realized and accomplished actor. Unfortunately, over time, he no longer returned my calls, and we lost touch. Although that pained me on many levels, I thought of him a while ago when my chain broke.

Unlike Reilly, when I moved to Los Angeles to pursue an acting career, and for many years after, I was chained to an image of *who I was*. And that image became as real as the cross that dangled from my neck. The tragedy is that the chain bound me to a frozen picture of *who I'd been*, keeping me from being someone *I might have become*.

When the chain broke, I relegated it to hanging from my bulletin board, affording me a distance that has only improved my vision. Ironically, the chain breaking has made it easier to release the cross of my dated ways as I embrace a new kind of symbol—a brilliant opportunity to become an unchained version of the me that is long overdue.

I would really enjoy that—cross my heart!

Unless and Until: Tim DeChristopher and the Infinite Egg

When I was in college, a friend of mine who was studying physics told me an interesting theory. It posited that if you dropped an infinite number of eggs off a two-story building, ultimately one of those eggs would not only *not* shatter on impact, but would actually bounce back to the point from which it was dropped. When I asked him where he would get an infinite number of eggs, he said he supposed from an infinite number of chickens. When I then asked him what came first, the infinite chickens or the infinite eggs, my friend looked like he wanted to drop me off a second-story ledge.

I mention this story to underscore my own benign sense of skepticism about pretty much everything. This isn't something I readily came to, this realization about my own doubt. And for all my resignation over my stance, I still *want* to believe.

But in the absence of the ability to move myself to action, I'm relegated to my routines and habits and the ruts they form. In those moments, change seems impossible. I conform to the image of the person I perceive myself to be, despite my need for something essential, for

100

that most intimate form of human revolution: the personal revolution within, waiting to be declared.

But, for me, that is a concept drained of all meaning. The revolution indeed won't be televised, if only because it's not going to happen. And every day becomes nothing more than a two-story drop off an edifice that bears my own name.

Unless and until...

ONE DECEMBER, I RECEIVED AN EMAIL soliciting money for a young man who, in an act of civil disobedience, infiltrated a government auction of gas and oil leases in Utah. His name was Tim DeChristopher; he was a 27-year-old college student. On the day in question, he was taking part in a protest of the aforementioned sale, an event that various environmental groups recognized for what it was—the Bush administration's version of a Blue Light Special in aisle six. (If you haven't been to a K-Mart in awhile, apparently aisle six is where oil and gas are stored, beneath Natural Treasures that we bestow with the title "National Park.")

When Tim arrived at the march, the mood was one of dark and grudging acceptance. The protesters were no more than countless eggs, all of them being dropped from a height guaranteed to dictate a messy and inevitable conclusion. After years of activism on behalf of the environment, Tim had reached that juncture in which his feelings intersected with his actions. He saw a gap, and in a flash of inspiration, he decided to fill it by going into the auction.

Once inside, he was asked if he was there to attend the auction, and, if so, whether he was going to be a bidder. He answered yes to both questions, was issued a bidder's paddle, and was directed into the auction.

Once there, he noticed that bidding had already commenced. Though he wanted to disrupt the auction, he didn't know exactly how best to do that: Should he make a speech? Or should he just scream his objection to the events unfolding around him? In that instant of not knowing what to do, Tim was just another egg, hurtling through space toward the ground, awaiting a foregone conclusion.

Wielding his bidder's paddle, he began bidding on land, driving up the price on numerous plots with a mere flick of his wrist. But that wasn't enough—he decided it was time to save the land *by actually winning the bids*. He went on to win thirteen plots of land, comprising twenty-two-thousand acres, at a total cost of 1.8 million dollars. Not surprisingly, he was detained by authorities.

The money that I contributed was to help cover the amount due to the Bureau of Land Management as an initial payment on the land Tim had won. My contribution was an illusory drop in a bottomless bucket, so I volunteered my services as a writer on Tim's behalf. I wrote a post for his website, but that, too, felt lacking.

So I began taking steps to align my feelings with my actions.

Although I was painfully aware that none of that felt revolutionary, I accepted it because of Tim's example and what it had taught me. In the past, whenever I thought of revolution, I would envision throngs of people, whipped into a frenzy, committing heroic acts to overthrow that which was wrong and outdated. And the plain truth of the matter is that for that group to exist, individuals within it must undergo their own personal revolution, one egg at a time.

Tim threw himself off a second-story ledge the day he bid on those parcels of land, much like he had been doing every time he acted on behalf of the environment. But this time he did it to save pristine red rock desert for generations to come. This time he did it to align his feelings with his actions. And in so doing, Tim didn't shatter—he bounced back.

Tim became the Infinite Egg!

The Department of the Interior voided the leases sold in the auction. Then the United States government indicted Tim, charging him with two felonies—violating the Federal Onshore Oil and Gas Leasing Reform Act, and making false statements. He was found guilty at trial and spent 21 months in prison.

I spoke with Tim before his indictment. I knew his own revolution was ongoing and that it sparked even more upheaval as forces gathered to support him and his efforts. Despite the myriad ways people endorsed his actions, Tim's biggest hope was that his efforts that day would spur others to their own revolution.

In a small way, I hope telling you this story is a step in that direction for us all. Studying Tim's example, I finally understand that *unless* we embrace our need for personal revolution, and *until* we are willing to align that need with real action, we're all just another egg, waiting for a bounce that we haven't yet earned.

Seeing Myself Through
Another Man's Windows

For ancient Greeks, the eyes were the windows to one's soul. One day, many years ago, I noticed my windows were clouded and lifeless...

It was early on a hot summer morning, and as I stared into the mirror over my bathroom sink, I was seized with the notion that my life had become nothing I recognized nor wanted. I had moved west to become an actor, and though I'd achieved modest success, none of it connected me to anything meaningful. All it led me to was this moment—working a nine-to-five job, angling my way through rush hour traffic, yearning for a cup of coffee.

I was wrestling with that realization when, out of nowhere, I looked up and suddenly saw an old man crossing the street in front of me. I hit the brakes, the tires screeching their protest. As startled as I was, though, the old man barely seemed to notice how close he'd come to becoming roadkill.

He was dressed in a dark suit and black fedora, more fitting for a Chicago winter than a midsummer Los Angeles morning. I shook my head at his carelessness as I parked the car and ran into Starbucks.

As I got in line, there he was again—the man I almost hit—right in front of me. I wanted to say something to him about being so negligent, but he turned to me first. "Hello," he said with warmth and familiarity, almost as if we were old friends. I felt disarmed, instantly regretting having had any ill thoughts about him. When he got to the head of the line, he ordered a cup of coffee.

"Tall, grande, or venti?" the clerk asked. The old man looked perplexed.

"Just a cup of coffee, please," he answered.

And in one of those moments that make you wish for a simpler time, the clerk recited the same inane litany of choices. Watching this was torture, so I stepped up and ordered a large cup of coffee for the old man. When he finally got what he came for, he exited the line, toasting me with a look of gratitude and a tip of his hat.

As I stirred my coffee, I noticed the old man had taken a seat on the patio, and that I would have to pass him on my way out. I looked up at the clock—I was running late—but as I exited the café, I inexplicably stopped and asked if I might join him. He effortlessly gestured to a chair, like he had been expecting me the entire time.

Sitting down, I finally got a good look at him. His suit was shiny from too much wear; his shoes clung to his bare feet with what little life they had left in them. The light blue shirt he wore beneath his coat was missing a button right over his heart. His expressionless face was rimmed by a thick gray beard, which gave way to his eyes: two deep pools of blue, an oasis in the desert of his parched countenance. I didn't really see his face until I saw his eyes.

His name was Sam. He was 72 years old and had suffered a stroke sometime in the last two years. He was Jewish, from Germany. He'd been married twice, with children from his first union. They were all adults now.

As we talked, Sam's words seeped through his lips like water from a dam straining not to burst. Yet the more he leaked, the greater the cascade. Listening to him, I was struck by the jagged paradox he posed: He was dressed shabbily, but he carried himself regally. And even when he became animated, I could detect him trying to maintain an air of decorum.

Then, in one of life's head-on coincidences, Sam began to talk about the very things that had weighed so heavily on me that very morning. He spoke about his past and how it didn't match up with his present. He didn't even bother to mention his future. In fact, the more he spoke, the more passive his voice and manner grew, until by the end of our conversation, he was talking as if his life was over, and he was merely marking the days. During the time it took me to finish my coffee, the craggy contradiction had become worn smooth with sadness, blanketed with resignation.

Getting up to leave, I asked if he needed a lift. Sam graciously accepted a ride to a cross-town bus stop. As I pulled over to the curb to drop him off, he sighed. "Can I tell you something personal?" he asked. I accepted his offer, thinking he was going to tell me that he knew it was me who'd almost hit him earlier that morning. But instead he took my hand between his, tattooing me with his stare.

"Michael, I'm old, and you may think I don't see much anymore, but when I look into your eyes, I see the eyes of one who can do anything. But, Michael, I also see one who is blind to all he has already done…"

Reflexively, I withdrew my hand, brushing away his kind words. But he firmly grabbed it back and continued speaking.

"Michael, I see the eyes of one who can do anything he wants!"

He then kissed my hand three times and was gone.

I would like to tell you that in the intervening years since I saw Sam that hot summer morning, my life has been transformed. That his vision propelled me to fulfill the promise he saw in my eyes. But that would be a lie neither of us could brook. What I can say with complete assurance and eternal gratitude, however, is that ever since that day, whenever I stare into the morning mirror, every once in awhile I see a glimpse of what I imagine Sam saw that day. And for the briefest instant, I believe it, too.

Which is deeply Greek to me.

Spring

Confessions of an Altared Boy

I was raised in the Greek Orthodox faith. I'm probably not the first person to observe that the Church and the theater are a lot alike. In fact, the road to my salvation as a kid led right down the middle of the intersection of the two.

To prove the point, my first acting job came by way of the Church. I was ten years old, and enrolled in the Greek school there, when we put up a play that was set in a barnyard. Unaware of the evils of typecasting, I was assigned the role of a piglet. As such, I had a monologue that, loosely translated, went something like this:

Today I am a piglet—tomorrow, with the grace of God, I might be sausage!"

The Church newsletter gave me a rave review: "Raysses brought sizzle to the role of the piglet, without ever toppling into hamminess—*soo-ie!*"

It was just the springboard I needed to get to the next rung within the Church hierarchy. Thus, I became an altar boy, a major player in the pomp and circumstance of the Greek Orthodox Church!

The job was intoxicating *and* intimidating: intoxicating because I got to wear a gold lame robe that lent me an angelic sheen…almost. Intimidating because I got the chance to work in close proximity to our priest, a gallows pole of a man we called "Father."

Now, I was taught that Father was God's representative here on Earth, which put a little distance between him and me—let's just say that I wanted to make a convert of him, because *everyone* loved my performance. Everyone, that is, *except Father...*

I reported for duty shortly thereafter. The liturgy began when the huge door that separated the altar from the congregation slowly opened to reveal Father. Draped in shimmering raiment, his back to the congregation, he would turn and start the service. That door slid open with a long, regal pull, like a curtain rising to start a show. And typically, it was the church sexton who opened it. But on my first Sunday, the sexton wasn't there; so, Father very subtly signaled me to slide the door open, instantly transforming me from Earth-bound imp into a sixty-pound-cherub-in-training.

Flushed with my lofty new status, I strode to the door, which dwarfed me. But on its sides were handles for me to latch onto as I did God's work—handles I gripped as if they were life itself. And when Father cued me, I uncoiled like a tightly wound spring bound for Heaven.

Unfortunately, no one had told me that the door was mounted on ball bearings and opened quite easily. Instead of the languid glide the congregation had come to expect, the door whipped open, sounding like a giant fishing reel with its drag still on. As it banged to a halt, I crashed to Earth in a pile of rumpled lamé. Looking up, I saw a mural of God on the ceiling, his right hand extended as if to help me up. Just then, Father thrust himself between God and me, his glaring stare exiling me to a place that rhymed with "hell." In that moment, I was beyond redemption.

But thankfully another incident of someone's absence provided me my shot at deliverance.

It was just a few weeks later, and I was back in the altar. Now, the Greek Orthodox service incorporates what's known as a chanter; beyond just chanting, he serves as the warm-up act for the choir. Our chanter was an unremarkable man in a remarkable kind of way: he was a little person, which wasn't remarkable at all. What *was* remarkable about him was his uncanny resemblance to Bela Lugosi of Dracula fame. It was something he did little to downplay. Indeed, it was something he went to great lengths to highlight. He dyed his hair jet-black, combing it aggressively straight back; he wore his little black robe *everywhere!* And his thick Greek accent sounded suspiciously Transylvanian to my ten-year-old ear.

All the altar boys called him Bela, though never to his face. It was just a pagan ritual that bound us all together.

Well, on this particular Sunday, we were at the part of the liturgy where Father would sing a short burst and Bela would chant his response. Things started out okay—Father sang his part—but there was no response from Bela...because he wasn't there. I saw Father pause and glance out toward Bela's podium, but he was greeted with nothing but stony silence. So Father continued singing up to another point where it was Bela's turn to respond, and again, no Bela!

At that point, both Father and I looked out at the empty podium. A look of consternation flashed across his face, putting a little starch in his collar, if you know what I mean. With his back to the congregation, Father angled his head in my direction and began silently mouthing words, words I couldn't hear. So I craned my head and cocked my ear, and, finally, I was able to make out what Father was trying to tell me:

"*Go get Bela!*"

Those words thundered in my ears—God's representative on Earth was calling Bela Bela!

In that moment, as Father became more human, in a weird way, God did, too. And I realized that maybe nirvana wasn't that far away, after all. Then again, what did I know? Tomorrow I might be sausage.

Getting Lost: Reflections From Under a Kitchen Table

> "I don't mind getting lost so long as I know where I'm at."
> —*My Uncle Tasso*

I've never been one to appreciate the middle of anything. Half-time entertainment and intermissions bore me. Middles of novels usually sag into an oblivion that leaves me in a stupor, praying for an eventual crescendo of literary fire.

My middling outlook, however, fits less snugly when applied to myself: I'm the second of three children. I'm ensconced in the midst of middle age. I am a bull's-eye walking along a median down the dreaded middle of Life's road.

Yet middle age is a great vantage point from which to view the margins to which I feel most naturally drawn: starts and finishes, beginnings and endings. From here, I can view my own beginnings; they include when I got lost, how I got found, and the blurry border where those two elusive states met.

Some of my earliest memories are as sharp as kittens' claws. Though I liked being around and playing with my cousins, I welcomed the chance to be alone, too. Only in solitude could I just sit and muse. Somehow, that felt special. I was also aware of being small for my age. Given my stature, it's no surprise that I had an affinity for the ground; it was, after all, never too far away.

Most Sunday afternoons, my family would go to my Uncle Nick's house. My father's eldest brother, Uncle Nick was the paterfamilias of my dad's side of the family. It was around an ancient table in his kitchen where my extended relatives would gather, crammed side by side, to feast on titanic meals of Hellenic delicacies prepared by my many various aunts. Afterwards, the kids dispersed as the adults commandeered the table.

It was a study in simple beauty, that table. It was porcelain-topped, embossed with an ornate design in the same shades of blue and white as those found in the Greek flag, and it ran the length of the kitchen itself.

After one such Sunday meal, when the children vanished to the park without me, I found myself back in the kitchen. The grown-ups were immersed in a round-table discussion I could best compare to a whirlpool— voices came from everywhere at once, making it hard for me to know who was saying what, which was totally beside the point. What really mattered was the vortex of energy that swirled around that room. I felt like it could lift me up and wash me away. So, unnoticed, I dropped to the floor and crawled under the table.

In my new world down there, my eyes adjusted to the outlines of feet that would shed their shoes and legs whose nylon stockings would end up in coiled cuffs during the course of the afternoon.

Inexplicably, isolating myself physically made it much

easier to tell who was saying what. I discovered that listening is a great method of seeing. The passion in my Uncle Nick's voice looked like the color red. As for my Aunt Doo-Doo (don't ask), her voice was all purple and gold, colors as gaudy as the dresses she wore.

But what really completed the *sous la table tableau* was the symphony emitted from those marathon melees atop the table. The porcelain had a range of tones when struck, whether by the flat of one of my uncle's hands offered as an exclamation point; or the rhythmic clicking of my aunts' fingernails, tapping out a Morse code signal of distress at being unable to contribute as freely as the men, something that bothered me even then.

But for all the laughter that volleyed over that table Sunday after Sunday, the conversation always seemed to end on a somber note. A deceased family member's name would be invoked, someone beloved and missed, and the din would dwindle till all I could hear was the woeful silence of tears streaking down cheeks. Inevitably, one of the men would sigh, "Yeah, well, what the hell you gonna do?" And with that, the party would be over.

AROUND THAT TIME, I was on a field trip to the Museum of Science and Industry with my fourth-grade class, when I found myself in a corridor as capacious as my curiosity. I drifted between the coal mine exhibit and the submarine display the entire afternoon, until I realized I had no way to find my pack of classmates. Panicked, I saw a booth with a banner that captured my dilemma to a tee: Lost and Found. When the elderly woman with glasses pinched onto the end of her nose asked if I needed help, I replied, "I'm lost. And I'd like to be found."

That experience introduced me to the idea of *getting lost* versus the state of *being lost*. When I drifted away from my classmates that day or when I crawled beneath the kitchen table, I was "getting lost," striking out to discover things on my own terms. "Being lost," on the other hand, was the sunken feeling I had when the exhilaration of having gotten lost receded.

Since then, I've come to view my life as a constant state of being both actively and passively lost—of not knowing. Sometimes the not knowing is crippling, and sometimes it's propulsive. But the upshot for me is now best expressed in a variant of the words I spoke so long ago: "I'm found. But I'd like to get lost." I wish no less for you.

Now get lost, will ya'?

Between Heaven and Helen's Half-Acre

I grew up in a small town in the Midwest that was anything but urban. Yet it wasn't really bucolic, either. So, as a kid, I didn't really have a direct relationship with the soil.

Actually, that's not entirely true—I would say that until I was in the seventh grade, I had a very tumultuous and intimate connection with the ground. It culminated in our meeting rather abruptly when a friend of mine and I, in an eerie foreshadowing of bungee jumping to come, cut off all of the elastic from our underwear, knotted it together, nailed it to the top of my family's garage, and jumped off the roof. Clinging to it with the zeal of the gravitationally challenged, thinking the flimsy bands of rubber and cotton would guarantee us a gentle landing, the ground knew better, holding itself resolutely against our descent. Terra was never more firma.

I also had many extended family members who were renowned for their abilities within the plant world. My grandmother, and a couple of aunts and uncles, allegedly made the Green Giant look like a desiccated lime wedge. But the best example of my family's pedigree was a great-aunt who lived with us for a spell when I was in high school.

Aunt Helen was old at a time in my life when dealing with her meant having to overcome my adolescent bias against the aged. (She also talked to her cat, Kukla, in a way that made me think she was actually conversing with it, which, over time, only made me love her more.) Aunt Helen's desire to communicate with non-human objects didn't end with her cat, though. She also talked to plants. Any plants. She would tour our backyard, picking up odd twigs and stems. She would find a dried-out husk of some fallen flower, and within a few days of water, sunlight, and a little coaxing in her native Greek, that shell would miraculously strike a deal with the devil and regain its life and vitality. She would then transplant it in some corner of the yard where even the birds left it alone, and by the following spring that discarded pod of vegetation had become something for us all to behold.

Aunt Helen's facility with all things green should have been all the proof my older sister needed to buttress her claim that my parents had secretly adopted me. You see, I inherited none of Aunt Helen's abilities. In fact, I lived at the other end of the herbal spectrum—my thumbs weren't green, they were black. And clumsy. As I grew older, though, I eased into my role as plant assassin. I became a horticultural hit man. The heartiest cactus withered at my mere touch. I was the guy people entrusted their plants to when they no longer wanted them around. Things hit rock bottom when a friend entrusted his Chia pet to me, only to have it devolve into a brown mass of what looked like mutant bean sprouts. This was cause for great consternation because, though I loved nature, that devotion never translated itself into anything even remotely green or life-sustaining.

Despite a potent disconnect with the plant world, though, I still think a lot about what I learned from Aunt Helen. Something I didn't realize until many years after the fact was the idea that a garden is a state of mind. Before I lived with Aunt Helen, I always saw gardens as articulated plots of land, there for the express purpose of planting, cultivating, and reaping what you had sown. They had little fences around them, and even the very ground had lines of demarcation announcing where the yard ended and the garden began.

But watching Aunt Helen traipse through nature, I discovered that the garden was everywhere and anywhere she put her intention. And even when one of her pet projects didn't bloom the way she wanted it to or for as long as she thought it should, she understood the intrinsic value of that plant's life in the bigger picture of a garden that only she could see.

So, despite my failings within the plant world, I've come to an understanding of my own garden—the one in my head. That whether I am aware of it or not, I am constantly planting, cultivating, and reaping the fruits of thoughts of all sorts. And that with a little intention, some sunlight, and coaxing, there really is no such thing as a dead notion. Unless, of course, I revisit the plan to cut off all the elastic from my underwear, tie it together, nail it to the top of my garage, and jump off. That's something that deserves to stay buried beneath the surface, never to take seed.

Sixty Seconds and a Pocketful of Change

The older I get, the more I feel the need to define the world as being made up of two contrasting factions. For instance, I used to think that the world broke down into two basic groups: those who believed the world broke down into two basic groups and those who didn't. Now I know the truth: the world breaks down between those people who make lists as a way of life and those who don't.

Generally speaking, I fall into the latter category. Although I feel like Christmas is an exception to the list rule for obvious reasons. You know, the Christmas List of all of those things that you wanted when you were young.

As a kid, I'd dissect the Sears catalog, meticulously logging every toy that caught my eye. I'd edit my list, lacing it with intricate insights to convey to Santa, as to which gifts were absolutely necessary and which ones were solely up to his discretion. One year, I actually tried to get letters of recommendation from my parents that substantiated my requests. To my mind, the letters would remind Santa of my sterling character and my impeccable conduct over the preceding year, that D I got in conduct notwithstanding.

I know you're thinking, "Somebody's inner-child needs a time out," but that's where you're mistaken. I've matured. I know better than to expect all of the items on my list to show up. Actually, that's only half-true. I still expect all of the things on my list to be there come Christmas morning. That's because I only want one thing: a mirror.

It may sound vain, but that's what I want. But not just any mirror. I'd like one that lies to me, so that when I peer into it, instead of splashing the image of a balding middle-aged man in my face, it reflected the picture I have in my mind: thin waist, thick hair that cascaded down, shading a pair of eyes that saw only the potential for what could be. A stiletto shadow that cleaved the light, dancing to rhythms that it heard in the night.

But that mirror doesn't exist.

So I confront the geezer in the glass. I look into his eyes. He looks backs. A smirk creeps over his face—or is it my face smirking and he's just taunting me? We recognize each other, nodding our hellos. Then, as he leans back, his manner shifts. His body poses the question neither of us wants to hear: "So, what have you got?" My eyes go south, and though you'd think his would too, they don't. His eyes become drills that bore into me.

The anesthesia of my youth has long since worn off and the drills have their way, slowly finding their mark. I look up and see oceans forming in his eyes, brimming and briny, poised to crash onto the shore of his face. And just as the squall is about to be born, it dies. The mountains of his shoulders sag. A sigh blows from a valley deep within me. He plunges his hands into his pockets, fingering the coins that live there. I hear their tinny chorus.

Change.

He winks. I wink back.

All we have is Change.

As I turn away from the mirror, though, I realize there is more. There's *the moment*—we also have that. So I turn back to share it with him. But the moment is over—he's already gone. And without even realizing it, I have just been given a most sacred gift: the awareness that all I have, all any of us has, is this moment. And a bottomless pocketful of Change.

And who knows? Maybe time will tell us that the greatest gifts truly are the ones that aren't on any list, but the ones you never see coming. Which, the more I think about it, isn't Greek to me at all.

The Ties That Bind

"Never trust a man who ties a double-Windsor.
He's overcompensating for something."
—*My Uncle Tasso*

On June 8, 2008, my father passed away after a long illness that made the last days of his life flicker and sputter like the flame from a blow-torch that had no fuel left to burn. He died 16 days after I'd returned to Los Angeles from a week we'd spent together. Throughout my entire stay, we both silently recognized that, in all likelihood, we would never see each other again.

When I went back to Indiana for the funeral, I felt a paradoxically palpable sense of emptiness: a vacuum so profound it filled the space with its nothingness.

Later, when all the well-wishers and extended family had gone, it was just my mom and me in the house where I grew up. She was sitting on the bed in Pop's room. The doors to his closet were open, and his clothes hung limply yet neatly.

As I heard the echo of Mom's memories caroming off the walls, I watched her eyes roam the floor as if she were looking for something, or at least trying to retrieve something that she'd seen the last time she was there.

Finally, she asked me if there was anything of Dad's that I wanted. (Though working class, my father prided himself on his formalwear and the accessories that accompanied it; there were watches, cuff links, belts, and handkerchiefs galore.) As much as I loved my Pop, though, I wanted none of it. Then, almost as an afterthought, Mom asked whether I wanted any of Dad's ties.

More than any of the items Pop wore, ties were his passion: they most tellingly illuminated dimensions of himself that he wasn't comfortable expressing more directly. There were single-hued ties in muted tones for somber affairs, like funerals and wakes. There were gaily adorned ties for Greek dances and dinners in Greektown. There were understated ties that subtly conveyed a regal sensibility, something I always marveled at because, though he never rose above a humble station in life, he carried himself like a benevolent king. What united this colorful flock of ties was that they were all top-shelf and expertly crafted.

Ties were also one of the things Pop used to connect with me as a young man. Learning to tie them required his expertise. It was a rite of passage I know he reveled in sharing. Although not an inherently patient man, when it came time to teach me to tie a tie, Pop really extended himself, understanding that to be short with me over my inability to duplicate a knot would risk losing one more thing that could bind us together.

That night in his room as I examined his ties, I came upon one that froze me in my tracks—it was a tie I'd forgotten about, one I'd purchased for him more than 30 years ago.

❧

I WAS IN MY LAST YEAR of law school and still living at home. I'd fallen in love with a girl I was dating, a woman much younger than me. And for some unknown reason, my father had an aversion to her that was so glaring it brought out things in him I had never seen before, moving my dad to behave in ways that made him a stranger to me. Up until that time, I'd never witnessed my father being anything but consummately polite to everyone; to him, proper decorum was a point of honor and dignity. Yet somehow this woman's presence in my life unnerved him so acutely that he exhibited a thinly veiled belligerence that violated everything he had ever stood for. That made him a hypocrite in my eyes, and it sent our relationship into a death spiral.

Exchanges between us swung violently between icy bursts and torrid thrusts. It got so bad that if the phone rang and I answered it and the call was for him and he was present, I would tell Mom it was for Pop, as if he wasn't sitting right there. Seeing the pain in Mom's eyes from being crushed between two stubborn, implacable forces made me understand that we had reached an impasse from which there was no turning back.

For the first time in my life, I addressed my dad not as my father but as a man. I told him that, although I didn't know much, I knew that if we continued on the path we were on we were going to inflict permanent damage on our relationship. He listened mutely, nodding when I'd finished, though offering no immediate response.

We eventually reconciled, though it came so gradually that time-lapse photography couldn't have captured it. When Father's Day approached, still smarting from our war but not wanting to be disrespectful, I bought him a tie for the occasion. But my heart wasn't in it. Sadly, my choice reflected that fact: I bought him a clunky knit tie that was as ugly as it was unfeeling. I never saw him wear it once.

And here it was now, though, 30 years later.

Pop treated his ties like he treated his friends—he would never let one go. Why he kept this one I can only guess. Perhaps it reminded him of how we can let relationships suffer in the presence of a love we thought was indestructible. I needed no such reminder.

I ended up taking three ties, each uniquely reflective of the man. And whenever I find the occasion to put one on now and begin to tie it, I hear his voice telling me to measure the ends, intersecting the short side with its longer counterpart, swinging it gently, looping it over itself, twisting it precisely so it doesn't wrinkle, pulling it through loops that weren't there a second ago, pressing my fingertips onto the newborn knot, tugging it gently but firmly into place as I pull its grip around my throat.

Sometimes when I cinch it too tightly and it feels like it's about to choke me, I think of how my love for Pop is a lot like the tie wrapped around my neck. It bends and it folds in ways I don't necessarily understand, clenching when it needs to, releasing when it must. But in the end what's important is how the tie ultimately comes to rest exactly where it should—over my heart.

How Green Was My Envy

"Envy is the art of counting the other fellow's blessings instead of your own."
—*Harold Coffin*

"I wish I had your sense of envy."
—*My Uncle Tasso*

I've never had my color chart done, so I have no idea what shade I most embody. I know that I've been angry enough to see red, been so depressed as to feel the blackest blue, and have written more than my share of purple prose.

But the color green poses an interesting dichotomy: Do I address it in its most recent incarnation as the *hue du jour* of those dedicated to returning the world to its most lush environmental tones? Or do I engage it based on the level of intimacy we've shared these many years? I plead no contest.

That's because I "went green" long before it was in vogue, polishing it to a lustrous jade. That is, assuming green is the color of envy, because if it is, I arguably qualify as the original not-so-jolly Green Giant.

As a young kid, I had a go-kart—or to put it more accurately, I had some decrepit two-by-fours that were joined together with rusty, repurposed nails, along with a used vegetable crate that I painted red and jury-rigged atop them. I affixed four wobbly lawnmower wheels to the two-by-fours, with the front two attached to a plank that swiveled from a creaky bolt. Attached to each end of the plank was a discarded length of clothesline, allowing me to steer by pulling to one side or the other. The entire contraption was powered by whomever I could entice to push me in exchange for returning the favor when it was their turn in the driver's seat.

Some time after I put my go-kart together, though, a close friend of mine got a real one—a motorized midget-racer with a fiberglass body. That mechanized magic carpet became all I could think about. After just one ride on his, mine became nothing more than a termite's wet dream. I remember literally aching as I gazed longingly at the object of my desire, wondering if I would one day have my very own.

Regrettably, I never did, leaving me to wrestle with an unquenchable impulse—the bottomless thirst left in Envy's wake.

As I got older, my affection for physical objects waned, replaced by a desire for things that other people had—as in "had accomplished."

When I first started acting, I had a friend who was a struggling stand-up comedian. We would commiserate over the frustrations of being poor, all the while jockeying for chances to perform, and the attendant insecurity those things gave birth to. He fell on some hard times, had his car repossessed, and needed money. So I hired him for an acting gig at a local high school in which we performed some play that's now long forgotten. It wasn't much, but it was something to keep the dogs at bay.

Years later, after we'd both moved to Los Angeles, his career began to take off. And very quickly, he started getting opportunities I had no access to because of his emerging status as a stand-up comedian. It was around that time that Envy re-entered my life; the green-eyed serpent had now become a vine that had twined itself from within, choking me from understanding myself.

Things spiraled in both directions. As my friend's career soared, mine floundered. Not surprisingly, anything I achieved during this time felt puny and inconsequential; even when I booked a role on the show that he starred in and produced, it felt resoundingly lacking.

Some time after that, I began to shift my focus to writing. A couple of years later, though we'd fallen out of touch, I interviewed him for a newspaper about a movie that he had starred in and was promoting.

Now, you might think that scenario would have weaned me from my pas-de-dux with Envy, but I had occasion to find out otherwise. While cruising through a local bookstore, there among the latest offerings I came across a book this very friend had written. It was put out by a big publishing house and was doing very well. I was sucked under in a riptide of resentment, drowning in waves of Envy.

Thankfully, my involvement with "going green" ran its course when I hit rock bottom that day. I realized that there was a way out of Envy's toxic thrall—and the answer, ironically enough, was to be found in the principles of genuine green living.

Author David Allen, in his book, *Getting Things Done*,

espouses the following tenets for living a verdant life: strive for simplicity; be fair; establish a relationship with your community; aspire to sustainability; assert a plan for your life; and conduct it with transparency.

Thinking back on my old go-kart, I realize it coincidentally embodied more than a few of those principles. It was a study in simplicity, fairness, and transparency. It cost virtually nothing to put together, moved whenever anyone wanted to swap a turn pushing for one driving, and was exactly what it held itself out to be—unalloyed, albeit bumpy, fun.

Obviously, it didn't deter me from my marathon run with Envy to come. Too bad Envy didn't combat male pattern baldness, didn't give me a flat stomach, or at least make me seem more worldly. At least now, though, I know a healthy green lifestyle is a viable option. I see people all around me creating it for themselves. My problem? I envy them, which is verdantly Greek to me.

Acting Like the Guy I Want to Be

Every year, tens of thousands of people move to Hollywood to pursue their dreams of becoming an actor. If they're anything like I was years ago when I unloaded all my worldly possessions from the cramped hatchback of a rusting Toyota into an even smaller apartment, they probably had visions of the kinds of roles they wanted to portray. I certainly did.

I even came up with character titles that embodied my fantasies: The Wacky Ethnic Guy. The Mercurial Ethnic Guy. And my favorite, the hybrid Wacky-But-Potentially-Mercurial Ethnic Guy. They all sprang to mind, never really impressing upon me their obvious similarity.

For the first year after I moved here, though, I wasn't offered a single role. So, not surprisingly, I jumped at the chance to play a small part in a large studio film. My character's name? Guy in Elevator.

Close enough. I was going to make my big screen debut in a Warner Brothers film called *Final Analysis,* starring Richard Gere, Kim Basinger, Eric Roberts, Uma Thurman, and Gary Oldman.

In the script, I was in a single scene that took place in an elevator; and though there were a couple of extras there, the scene involved just Gary and me. As we were introduced to each other, I remembered thinking that I must be at least a decent actor because I wasn't acting one bit nervous about working with a man whose dramatic gifts were daunting to anyone, especially a newcomer like myself. So I acted calmly because implicitly I knew that I couldn't act with someone if I was intimidated by them or their talent. Essentially, I needed to act like me.

So I got to the studio bright and early, and, as it turned out, the very first shot of the day was my scene with Gary—with a twist: my close-up was the first shot up. I was flattered—*I* got to go *first*. Later, I found out that this is standard procedure: when a scene is being shot between a star and a lesser actor, they give the star more time to practice the scene before flipping the camera around for his close-up.

Not a problem, I thought; I welcomed the chance to flex my untested thespianic muscles. Before I knew what was really happening, though, I was on set, the sticks were up, and we were rolling.

In a swirl of noise and motion, we did a first take so quickly that I was left feeling like a spun top. Not being actor enough, that fact must have clearly registered on my face; just as we were about to do a second take, Oldman, who up until that moment had positioned himself on the camera's base so he could pinch his face up next to its lens as he delivered his lines to me, leaned in and whispered in my ear, "This is really hard to do first thing in the morning—you're doing great!"

I don't know that I've ever wanted to kiss a man more, but in that instant he validated what I was feeling, liberating me to excel, which, thankfully, I did.

Later, when we broke for lunch, Gary asked me to join him, and I gladly accepted, thinking we'd eat in his trailer. But he wanted to eat on the studio lot instead. So we went to a concession stand and ate while sitting at a picnic table. In a slow-motion blur, tourists drifted by, staring at us, introducing me to a phenomenon I'd been previously unaware of: fame's gravitational pull and the resultant distortional effect.

Once they spotted Oldman, people would get pulled in, craning their necks to see him, thinking, *Gee, that looks like Gary Oldman... sitting with...no one famous.* After they'd see me, I'd watch their features go limp when it became apparent to them that, though they thought they had seen Gary Oldman, because I was no one they recognized, my absolute lack of fame eclipsed any possibility that they may have actually seen a genuine celebrity. Ironically enough, all of this left me with a case of existential whiplash.

While we ate, I got the urge to confess how over my head I'd felt earlier that morning, having working class roots and never having formally studied acting. But just then Oldman launched into a story, telling me about his childhood. How he grew up in a home that didn't have as much as an indoor toilet. He didn't even step foot in a restaurant until the he was sixteen. But all that changed when he made his screen debut in the independent film, *Sid and Nancy.*

Virtually overnight, he went from being an un-known struggling actor to becoming Gary Oldman, Famous Actor Guy—jetting around the world, marrying Uma Thurman. Suddenly all of these people were now clamoring to hear what he thought on any given topic, merely because of his newfound status as a bona fide international movie star. And the entire time, he told me, all he wanted to do was scream into their faces, because he knew not one of them would've given him the time of day if he hadn't been plucked from obscurity by dint of Lady Luck's random touch.

I wanted to tell him that somehow, in my own way, I understood what he was talking about, but I decided against it. I was too bowled over by how closely his path hewed to mine.

From then on, all the images of the various characters I'd devised were drained of any meaning for me. Instead, I began to contemplate a role that had never really crossed my mind until that moment—*myself.* I could just choose to be me. Because isn't that every human being's ultimate role, actor or otherwise—to find themselves, to play themselves, to figure out who they are, while living with the consequences?

And if that's hard for you to do, try *acting* like you understand. Take it from an Ethnic Guy Who Knows— you just may be pleasantly surprised.

IN A BIT OF A POSTSCRIPT, when we were done shooting that day, Gary came up to me, gave me a big hug, and said we must stay in touch so we could get together down the road. He turned and walked away without giving me the means to reach him, though.

Years later, I wrote about our experience and sold it to the *Los Angeles Times* Sunday Magazine. On the day it was published, I was flushed with pride and accomplishment; so much so, that I treated a friend to brunch at one of the expensive hotels down on the beach in Santa Monica.

After we ate, we were out walking on a bike path that ran parallel to the water; I was in my own private Idaho, when I saw my friend staring at a man who'd just strolled by in the opposite direction. She said, "Did you see who that was?—that was *Gary Oldman!*"

You may wonder why I didn't turn around and go catch up with him, and the plain truth is: It was too Greek, even to me…

The Song is Over

My earliest childhood memories are of sounds. I grew up in a household where extended family either lived with us or were constantly circulating through. The clatter of dishes being washed, the inimitable bang of a coffee pot being slapped on the stove, the chorus of voices that wafted from the kitchen, all raised in an effort to jumpstart the day.

At some point, those noises became ordered, even melodic. And soon they led me to a lifelong love affair with music before I consciously knew what music was: a swarm of invisible bees perpetually pollinating the flowers planted inside my young head, creating an eternal Spring within me.

Music's lure was so strong for me that it became irresistibly visceral. I remember a Saturday night when I couldn't have been more than five, hearing amplified music drift from the parking lot behind the church at the end of my street. As it turned out, I was hearing the strains of a sock-hop, where the dance floor was nothing more than a slab of asphalt. Somehow I talked my mom into dressing me in my sartorial finest (brown corduroy pants with an elastic waistband, paired with a shirt that I ultimately learned was a faux-paisley print), so that I could walk to the end of the block and sit on the curb directly across from the parking lot, my feet strumming the drainage grid in rhythm to the songs I was hearing, while I peered through the chain link fence at the garden of Eden on the other side.

From then, it wasn't long before I learned that the William Tell Overture (which was also the theme song of *The Lone Ranger* television show) could literally catapult me to my feet whenever I heard it. I'd race around, bouncing off of furniture, unwittingly doing my version of parkour, an impish colt trying to break free from a stable only it saw. The funny thing was that my family observed all of this, too. In fact, there were times when entertainment was so scarce that they would play the Overture on the phonograph, if only to watch the gyrations it produced in me. With no thought of their expectation, I never disappointed them.

Later, though, my personal music appreciation was transformed by the act of seeing it performed live. As moving as pure sound could be, there was something about seeing that sound created that lent a dimension to it that enlarged the song, made it more than it had been before. Now when I heard a note of death-defying clarity, I had the image of what it took to create that sound, whether it came from a guitar or a trumpet or a drum, and what the musician looked like producing it. It infused what I was hearing with a sense of humanity, so that I understood that the sound was not some abstract phenomenon but the result of a very real, palpable effort.

This equation was indelibly set on its ear back in 1975; I attended a Who concert at the Chicago Stadium, a venue designed for sports events, not concerts. Yet there I was, third row, main floor, standing on my chair, in front of my idol, guitarist Pete Townsend. Looking up at him, awash in the froth thrown off by the power chords he dispatched like Zeus's lightning bolts, I saw a look of such unspeakable beatitude on his face as he gazed out onto the throng that I had to know what made him so luminous, so powerful.

Instinctively, I turned around to see what he was seeing, and just as I caught a glimpse of the people facing him, I was blown off my chair. I literally fell down, as if I had stepped into a spiritual jet-stream born of the torrent of energy that came thundering off the people who'd gathered there. It was life-altering: the crowd was the source of Townsend's state of being. Or was it? I couldn't tell any more.

Driving home that night was a revelation. The lines between creator and created, audience and auditory, all merged and blurred, leaving me to understand (suspect?) that the stage is just one factor in the inscrutable equation of creativity's existence and thrall. After witnessing what I'd just seen, I remember thinking that I wanted to be both the cause and the effect, as well as the recipient, of Creativity's dividend.

But music wasn't my mode of expression. For a while, acting was. Yet as I got older, speaking other people's words felt less fulfilling, with few exceptions. So I started to write, and as I became more comfortable with doing so, I learned that the words I wanted to speak had to be mine. There was a directness, a tightness of fit, that made that my only viable option.

I have had the good fortune to write for a living on and off throughout my life. At one point I spent six years writing a regular column for a journal called *Vision* magazine. It was a joy, that gig, until one day when it was no longer: The magazine told me it was heading in a new direction, and, apparently, I was, too. I typically respond to change much in the same way most people do to getting kicked in the shin—it's nothing I welcome, and my default reflex is almost always one of rabid resistance. Although I flinched when I was told this news, I knew it was for the best, and here's why:

I never know what's next for me as a writer, but what I do know is this: that I write for you, the reader. Granted, though I explore issues that intrigue me, beguile me, or confound me, I do so with the hope that these things have somewhat the same impact on you. And that by writing about them, I shed light on them, make them a little less mysterious, less daunting, or at least something you can put your arms around and conquer in your own time and fashion.

During that time with *Vision*, I was blessed with emails from readers that consistently buoyed my waning spirits. Sometimes those messages weren't necessarily of praise, but it didn't matter. Just the act of reaching out meant that someone, somewhere, had been moved to communicate something in response. And for this writer, that's as good as it gets.

I've always strived to write things worthy of my readers' time and effort; and so I devoted my last column for *Vision* to the act of expressing gratitude.

"If you've ever read any of my columns," I wrote, "I thank you. If you've reached out, bless you for taking the time to do so. I urge you to never forget the role that you, the reader, play in the ongoing dialogue that exists between you and any writer whose work you engage with. It's necessary and sacred and vital.

"For now, though, this song is over," I concluded. "And if that's Greek to you, that's more than good enough for me."

Epilogue: Elegy for a Greek Uncle

Life is a strange and wondrous thing.

Memorializing a muse is inherently difficult: Balancing grief, loss, and the desire to do right by the deceased requires a steady hand, a clear eye, and a brimming heart. It's made a lot more difficult when the person who's died never lived outside one's imagination.

Permit me to back up.

When I was in kindergarten, my mother had a parent-teacher conference in which she was commended for having me learn to play the violin. When Mom replied that I didn't play the violin, my teacher said, "That's odd—Mrs. Kagel says Michael is doing so well!" When Mom asked my teacher who Mrs. Kagel was, she answered, "Michael's violin teacher, the widow."

There was no Mrs. Kagel, no violin. What there was was a burgeoning imagination in me, bursting to populate the desert that was my inner landscape as a child.

Even then, I liked to make shit up.

"TASSO BOUBOULAKIS" FIRST appeared in a screenplay I wrote back in the '80s, entitled *Divine Intervention*. In it, he was a world-class raconteur-globetrotter-novelist, more renowned for his extravagant lifestyle than for his literary output. Although he died while in the middle of penning his magnum opus, he returned from the dead to enlist his estranged son to ghostwrite the remainder of the novel. Both characters were flip sides of the coin that was me, and they shared two pronounced traits: vast stores of unrealized potential and a constitutional inability to ever ask for help.

Ancient Greek poets drew inspiration from the likes of the enchanting Muse Calliope; I wound up with a lumpy Greek septuagenarian.

Maybe I could introduce Tasso to Mrs. Kagel…

YEARS LATER, WHEN I BEGAN writing my "Greek to Me" column for various outlets, I was working on a dead-end piece with no visible way out. I needed a combination backstop/trampoline; someone I could bounce ideas off while providing some firm pushback against my literary excesses. From some forgotten fold in my memory, Tasso's name rolled off my tongue, perfectly formed.

But he had evolved from his debut appearance in my screenplay: he'd aged gracefully, coming to an understanding and acceptance of himself that emitted a warm glow, like some familial campfire that made me just want to sit beside him. In other words, he morphed into the definitive "Greek Uncle"—accessible, inquisitive, and invested without infesting. He became so prominent in my consciousness that I began to insert him into my work regularly, to great effect. Readers responded viscerally to Tasso's appearances, praising his wit and wisdom.

Thus, Uncle Tasso became my go-to: If there was something I wasn't comfortable saying on the page, it was his to speak. If there was a quip that could somehow be sharpened by coming from the wizened lips of an aged, retired, working class man, he stepped into the breach. We had reached an exquisite equilibrium, Uncle Tasso and me—collaborators, comrades, partners in crime.

And then I betrayed him.

THREE YEARS AGO, I WAS floundering desperately: Living by myself, inching closer to undesired retirement, and having moved to a community where I knew no one, I found myself scraping the wall. Acute depression is always an uninvited houseguest, and mine was especially invasive. Clearly, I needed help but was incapable of admitting as much.

I had a close friend who for years had suggested a fellowship group to me, the ACA&DF—the Adult Children of Alcoholics and Dysfunctional Families. Posed with staring my own self-inflicted demise in its cold, blank face, I went to my first meeting.

Two years later, after countless meetings, I formally addressed the group by sharing my journey with them. Wanting to present myself accurately, I brought some pieces of mine to read, one of which, "Waiting for Tasso," appears in this book.

Reciting the story brought out the actor in me; I had a keen sense of the audience embracing Uncle Tasso, which at first elated me. But as I continued, I became soaked in an icy subterranean torrent that not only made it impossible to speak, but by the end of the reading, left me sobbing uncontrollably, along with some members of the group.

At that point, I confessed that Tasso wasn't real. That he didn't exist. That I had created him to utter words that I couldn't say; and that even when those words were honorable and praiseworthy, I couldn't speak them because I didn't feel worthy of them.

In the ACA paradigm, there are two key foundational concepts to be engaged on the road to one's recovery: the Inner Child/True Self and the Kind, Loving Parent. While reading that essay, Uncle Tasso revealed himself to me to be a hybrid of the two. As such, I had to expose the fiction that Uncle Tasso was so I could celebrate his greater truth to me by stepping out of his shadow.

IN THE PREFACE OF THIS BOOK, I stated that writing has always required of me an act of faith, a leap into a void of arguably my own creation. Over time, it has moved me to understand that I am the void, and writing was my way of defining myself to myself, of filling the emptiness, one piece at a time.

My experience wrangling words while grafting them to thoughts and mating them to feelings has paid myriad dividends, the nature of which could only have been gained by going through the requisite endless sifting and winnowing.

Writing is hard. Rewriting is harder. Honesty is hardest.

Initially, the highest compliment a reader could bestow on me was to tell me what a fine writer I was. But today, the most satisfying reaction I can get is when a reader says my words triggered some memory of their own—that by sharing my experience, I had prompted them to relive theirs, possibly in a new, expanded light.

But the most consequential revelation of compiling this anthology has been to magnify the individual pieces so that, for me, they have merged into an impressionistic mosaic of a life as random and whimsical as it is hope-fully engaging. A kind of inadvertent memoir.

My hope for you, dear reader, is that as the result of reading this book, you'll be moved to review your own life's stories, making connections that might have gone otherwise unnoticed. Thus, in the best way possible, making them Greek to you.

ACKNOWLEDGEMENTS

I WOULD LIKE TO EXPRESSLY THANK and acknowledge the following people for their generous support in the creation of this book. I literally couldn't have done it without you: Tony Krizman, Jill Nani, Bruce Kluger, Karen Griffith, Jim Benson, Donna Erwin, Gio Giovanni, Lorin Zerah, Bo Kane, Beth Fahey, Tasso Bouboulakis, Eric Karten, Sondra Birkenes, Steve Pressfield, the late Sydney Murray, Don Ray, Kimberly Wolfe, Desmond Oon, and Barry Newman, as well as the countless people who encouraged me along the way.

I would also like to acknowledge the contribution of the fellowship group, the ACA&DF (Adult Children of Alcoholics and Dysfunctional Families) to my life. This version of the book would not have been possible without the emotional sobriety it has brought me.

ABOUT THE AUTHOR

Born in Gary, Indiana, and after practicing law for a year in Chicago, Michael Raysses moved to Los Angeles in 1989 to pursue an acting career. His experience in that realm led him to become a word wrangler, culminating with the debut of his "Greek to Me" column in 2002, and running through 2013. This is his second book.

Self-Portrait by the author. Ink on paper. 1974.

Made in United States
North Haven, CT
19 December 2024